Praise for *The Champions Network*

"*The Champions Network* is a step-by-step guide for those trying to win hearts and minds in any organization. Matt uses case studies and insights into how organizations actually work to show how anyone can make impactful change. Professionals tasked with building culture will find this book particularly helpful."

David Searle, former Chief Ethics and
Compliance Officer, Walmart International

"*The Champions Network* will be mandatory reading for all my clients! The methodical roadmap that Matt Silverman provides is the ultimate (and only) pragmatic guide leaders with BIG IDEAS need. Matt not only addresses the steps needed but gives practical templates so you can quickly develop a network in your organization without reinventing the wheel."

Ellen C. Smith, JD, President, Amalie Trade Compliance
Consulting, former Vice President, Baker Hughes

"You've heard the expression, 'Anything worth doing can rarely be done alone.' *The Champions Network* provides an innovative and practical blueprint to getting things done inside your company, in your industry, and in the community at large. The concepts are sound and the examples bring everything to life. Highly recommended!"

Bill Cates, CSP, CPAE,
author of *Radical Relevance* and *Beyond Referrals*

"Matt Silverman's *The Champions Network* is your go-to guide for enhancing your organization's compliance program with internal influencers. Effective corporate compliance requires continuous commitment, improvement, and evangelism. Creating a network of compliance champions will extend the reach of your program and further protect the enterprise from financial, litigation, and reputational risk. I'm not the only one saying this. The Department of Justice's *Evaluation of Corporate Compliance Programs* now opines on the value of compliance champions!"

Martin T. Biegelman,
Managing Director at SunHawk Consulting and former
Director of Financial Integrity at Microsoft Corporation

"For people with enormous visions and unrelenting appetites to do good, this book is an absolute necessity! Matt's blueprint gives your big idea roots and legs. I invite you to build your champions network at work and in your community to spread the Veteran Champion Movement and 'be a part of the win.'"

Kathy Lowrey Gallowitz, Lt. Col., USAF, Retired,
author of *Beyond "Thank You for Your Service,"*
The Veteran Champion Handbook for Civilians

"Matt provides a well-reasoned approach to how we can all better communicate and spread ideas in our organizations. Whether you're looking to build a champions network or find effective approaches to influence others, this book provides key insights, research, and sound guidance to get you there."

Amy Eliza Wong, author of the critically acclaimed
Living on Purpose: Five Deliberate Choices to Realize Fulfillment and Joy

"Finally, a book that guides us through the process of starting and running a champions network. Matt clearly describes all the essential steps in establishing a champions network, whether it's for compliance and ethics, ESG, or any other purpose, written in a nicely-paced and practical style. An excellent addition to any compliance professional's library."

Gerry Zack, CEO, Society of Corporate Compliance and Ethics & Health Care Compliance Association

"Matt Silverman's blueprint for building a champions network is easy to understand and put into place. Success stories are described, demonstrating that time and effort invested in these networks pay off. With government agencies and organizations more concerned than ever about implementing good ideas for better culture, compliance, and ethics, why wouldn't you build one?"

Teri Quimby, JD, LLM, President of Quimby Consulting Group, board director, speaker, author, and former state regulator

"In *The Champions Network,* Matt Silverman expertly lays out a simple, adaptable, and powerful concept (and blueprint) that virtually any organization may want to consider deploying. *The Champions Network* is refreshing and empowering. It avoids the linguistic contortions and reframing of known concepts often present in the new business idea du jour that organizations adopt. Matt shows us that deploying champions networks is doable and perhaps a human antidote to the challenge of living in a time of diffuse information and communication challenges."

Robert V. Schnitz, former Senior Vice President and Chief Privacy Officer, Hyatt Hotels Corporation

THE CHAMPIONS NETWORK

A Blueprint to **EXPAND YOUR INFLUENCE** and **SPREAD BIG IDEAS** in Any Organization

MATT SILVERMAN

Published by
Ignite Press
55 Shaw Avenue #204
Clovis, CA 93612
www.IgnitePress.us

ISBN: 978-1-956531-10-7
ISBN: 978-1-956531-11-4 (Hardcover)
ISBN: 978-1-956531-12-1 (E-book)

For bulk purchases and for booking, contact:

Matt Silverman
matt@blueprintorg.com
https://mattsblueprint.com
https://blueprintorg.com

Library of Congress Control Number: 2023912041

Cover design by Mohtasim Mahmud and Martin Veleski
Edited by Elizabeth Arterberry
Interior design by Jetlaunch
Illustrations by Martin Veleski
Logo Design by Martin Veleski
Author Photographs © Geoff Reed

FIRST EDITION

This book is dedicated to the memory of my friend, Bradley Richards, and my grandmother, Flora Silverman

Avid readers and kind souls

ACKNOWLEDGMENTS

I'm grateful to all those who helped make this book possible.

To the team at Ignite Press, for their advice and hard work throughout the publishing process. While I hope I wasn't their most difficult client, I'm sure I wasn't their easiest.

To irreplaceable friends, family, and colleagues who took the time to help me improve this book, most notably: Martin Biegelman, Sarah Brackett, Juliette Gust, Katherine McIntosh, Teri Quimby, Robert Schnitz, Bonnie Silverman, Ron Silverman, and Ellen Smith.

To my family, for their patience and encouragement.

CONTENTS

Introduction xiii

Part I: The Background

Chapter 1: The Psychology of a Champions Network. 3
Chapter 2: What Is a Champions Network? 13

Part II: The Blueprint

Chapter 3: Gaining Leadership Commitment. 27
Chapter 4: Creating the Network Structure. 35
Chapter 5: Recruiting the Champions 45
Chapter 6: Training the Champions. 55
Chapter 7: Implementing the Network 65
Chapter 8: Measuring Network Success 79

Part III: The Examples

Chapter 9: Compliance and Ethics 85
Chapter 10: Health and Wellness 105
Chapter 11: Environmental and Social Responsibility 127
Chapter 12: Employee Recruitment and Retention 139

Conclusion. 145
Resources. 147
About the Author 155
Looking to Build a Champions Network? 156
Book Matt Silverman to Speak. 157
How You Can Champion This Book. 158

"Your job is to get your audience to care about your obsessions."

MARTIN SCORSESE, FILM DIRECTOR

INTRODUCTION

This is a self-help book.

That genre is usually reserved for books about ways to overcome personal problems: bad habits, negative thinking, unhealthy relationships, emotional instability, or struggles with growth, happiness, finances, or fulfillment. This is a different kind of self-help book that aims to solve a different kind of personal problem:

No one cares about your ideas.

Your ideas are brilliant and transformative. Your ideas would make everyone's life easier, solve organizational headaches and bottlenecks, reinforce a positive corporate culture, and help to achieve your professional goals. Your ideas might even make the world a better place.

No one cares.

People don't care about your ideas for one of two reasons: they don't know about them, or they haven't been convinced of their value. At least, not *yet*.

This book provides a blueprint to expand your influence in ways that ensure others know about your big ideas, find value in them, and support and spread them throughout your organization or community. This book differs from a traditional self-help book in that you don't need to do everything *yourself* to achieve the desired results. While there is plenty of work to be done on your end, the blueprint provided also requires action and accountability on the part of others: your *champions*.

Influencing others is not easy. It was hard enough before a global pandemic, when remote work was the exception, not the rule. The interpersonal networks that had developed organically in the workplace have faded in many respects. The blueprint in this book makes up for some of what we have lost in a post-COVID world.

While influencing others isn't easy, its relevance and impact in today's world can't be overstated. In the words of Harvard University instructor, author, and keynote speaker Carmine Gallo:

> *"Ideas are the currency of the twenty-first century. The ability to persuade, to change hearts and minds, is perhaps the single greatest skill that will give you a competitive edge in the knowledge economy—an age where ideas matter more than ever. . . As our economy has evolved from an agrarian to an industrial to a knowledge-based one, successful people in nearly every profession have become those capable of convincing others to take action on their ideas."*

This book is written for the individual or team looking to influence others to take action on their ideas by utilizing a champions network. While you can find articles and anecdotes online about developing champions networks, nothing I found in my research or in my years of working within such networks provided comprehensive guidance on how to build a successful champions network. This book was born out of the same necessity as so many others: it didn't exist, but it needed to. Now it does.

As you read, you may think from time to time: *"That concept or piece of advice sounds great in theory, but we don't have the budget, the time, or the management commitment."* It's rare that champions networks are implemented with all the desired pieces in place. Whether you're building a new network or improving an existing one, don't be concerned with fitting an exact mold or getting everything you want. Use the guidance and examples in this book to build a champions network that meets *your* goals and that's right for *your* organization or community. Where it makes sense to do so, prioritize and adjust accordingly.

This book begins with an analysis of why a champions network is an optimal model to expand your influence and spread big ideas, drawing on over 100 years of social science and psychological research. It continues by providing a background of what a champions network is and how it may benefit your organization. The next section provides the six-step blueprint to building a successful champions network, including how to:

- Gain leadership commitment and support.
- Create an organized and efficient network structure.
- Recruit the right champions for your network.
- Train your champions on their roles and responsibilities.
- Implement the network and adjust along the way.
- Develop metrics that demonstrate network success.

Because champions networks vary in their functions and forms, this book examines four different types of champions networks—compliance and ethics, health and wellness, environmental and social responsibility, and employee recruitment and retention—with real-world examples provided for each.

Why a blueprint? A blueprint is the foundational element of any construction project. It provides a vision for how the building is expected to look upon completion, along with a detailed plan for how to achieve the desired results. However, a blueprint can change as a project evolves, leaving room for "structural creativity" on the part of the architect. You're the architect of your champions network—follow the guidance in this book, but be flexible as you adapt it to your organization and goals.

Best of luck in building *your* champions network!

MATT SILVERMAN

PART I

THE BACKGROUND

"Nothing is as powerful as an idea whose time has come."

Victor Hugo, French Writer

1

THE PSYCHOLOGY OF A CHAMPIONS NETWORK

There are *many* ways to spread ideas. Drive down the road and you'll spot billboards. Turn on your television and you'll see advertisements. The internet is full of "influencers" trying to convince us to adopt the latest trend or buy the newest product. At work, you're likely to receive mass emails every day, or sit through company-wide meetings, or receive a visit every now and again from an outside consultant.

Even though it happens every day, it's not *always* successful. Some methods and models are more effective than others. *Why do some ideas spread like wildfire, while others take time to catch on, or fail to be adopted altogether?* That's the question this chapter answers, by analyzing the underlying psychology and behavioral science behind the spread of ideas and why we are influenced by some ideas more than others. With an understanding of the psychology behind the spread of ideas, you'll see why a champions network is an optimal method and model by which to expand your influence and spread *your* big ideas.

To understand how ideas spread, we have to go back almost 100 years and start in an unlikely place: the cornfields of Iowa.

THE DIFFUSION OF INNOVATIONS

The Iowa Hybrid Seed Corn Study

In 1938, Bryce Ryan, PhD, went to Ames, Iowa, and set in motion an entire field of academic research that continues to this day.

Ames was (and still is) the home of Iowa State University. As an agricultural and research university, Iowa State had played a vital role in the development of an innovation known as hybrid seed corn. Entire books have been written on the impact of hybrid seed corn, but here's all you need to know: hybrid seed corn revolutionized the agricultural world, allowing farmers to increase corn yields by about 20 percent per acre. Hybrid seed corn was introduced to Iowa farming communities around 1920, but it didn't become widely used by Iowa farmers until the early 1930s.

It had taken over a decade to catch on. *Why?*

Ryan gathered data from personal interviews with farmers in rural Iowa communities. He wanted to understand not only why it took so long for Iowa farmers to plant hybrid seed in their fields, but, just as importantly, to understand the factors that ultimately led to the widespread adoption of this practice.

Ryan's studies found that while many farmers were first introduced to hybrid seed corn through outside sources (commercial seed dealers and salespeople were mentioned in their interviews as the most significant sources of farmers' initial awareness of the innovation), what ultimately convinced farmers to adopt the use of hybrid seeds was their social networks: other farmers, neighbors, and trusted friends. Their interpersonal relationships and recommendations from peers were the deciding factors for so many Iowa farmers to begin planting hybrid seed—much more so than any outside influences.

Ryan's hybrid seed corn study would come to form the basis of a field of research known as "the diffusion of innovations." *Diffusion* is the process by which an innovation (a new idea or practice) is communicated through certain channels over time among members of a social system. "The diffusion of innovations" is a more formal and academic way of saying "the spread of ideas."

The hybrid seed corn study that was conducted by Ryan and his team was one of the first to demonstrate that interpersonal communication with trusted peers was a deciding factor in persuading individuals to adopt an idea and spread it within their social network. This isn't to say that experts, media, or other outside forces don't play a role in creating initial awareness, but ultimately, the diffusion of innovations model places emphasis on interpersonal communications with one's peers in creating influence and successfully spreading ideas.

Ryan's studies in Ames were followed up after World War II with numerous diffusion of innovations studies, particularly by rural sociologists at universities in the midwestern United States who had been influenced by Ryan's research at Iowa State. By 1960, numerous diffusion publications had appeared, with the largest number authored by rural sociologists. Most notably, the sociologist Everett Rogers popularized diffusion of innovations research in the 1960s through his S-curve theory, demonstrating that it takes only 10 to 20 percent of a social system (referred to as "early adopters") to initially adopt an idea and thereafter influence the majority of the social system to adopt it.

Diffusion research continued to spread (no pun intended) into the fields of economics, psychology, political science, engineering, education, communication, medicine, and marketing. By mid-2007, an estimated 6,000 diffusion studies had been conducted and published across numerous fields of study—all of which, in some way, were born out of Ryan's initial research conducted in the cornfields of Iowa.

Below are examples of three studies that incorporated the diffusion of innovations model.

Study #1: The Diffusion of Tetracycline

In 1966, a study was conducted among a sampling of physicians of a new medical drug named tetracycline. The study had been initiated by the pharmaceutical company Pfizer, which approached three sociologists with a request to determine the effectiveness of its tetracycline advertising in medical journals. The research gathered data from personal interviews with almost all the medical doctors in four small communities in Illinois.

The study showed that approximately seventeen months elapsed from the time doctors became aware of tetracycline to the time they began prescribing it to their patients. While medical journal articles and sales reps were important in creating initial awareness of the new drug, the study found that interpersonal communication among the doctors was *most* influential in their decision to begin prescribing the drug.

The research also found that doctors who were part of interpersonal medical networks adopted the innovation (i.e., began prescribing the drug to their patients) more rapidly than doctors who were more isolated in their medical practice. Tetracycline had been scientifically evaluated in numerous published clinical trials, and Pfizer salespeople had given the doctors free samples of tetracycline. However, the study showed that doctors chose to prescribe the drug mainly because of the personal experiences of their fellow doctors, as opposed to any outside influences.

Study #2: The STOP AIDS Program

In 1992, almost half of the gay community in San Francisco was HIV-positive. Gay organizations in the city began a grassroots movement to fight the HIV/AIDS epidemic through the STOP AIDS program. Focus group interviews were initially conducted by STOP AIDS to assess how much gay men already knew about the epidemic. Gradually, the STOP AIDS founders realized that the focus group interviews were having a strong educational effect on the participants as the group members exchanged useful information about HIV prevention. Men were recruited on the streets of gay neighborhoods in San Francisco to attend the small group meetings that were organized and led by outreach workers in the community.

The success of the STOP AIDS program relied heavily on diffusion theory: early adopters of the movement who made up a relatively small segment of the population initiated a new behavior that spread throughout the population. A well-respected individual who was HIV-positive led small groups of a dozen or so gay men. The transmission of the virus was explained, and individuals were urged to use protection or seek monogamous partnerships. Questions were asked and answers were discussed by the group. At the conclusion of the meetings, each member made a commitment to safer sex and to organize future small group meetings.

The STOP AIDS program was deemed successful in bringing about a large-scale change in the sexual behavior of gay men in San Francisco, in part because of the diffusion principles and communication strategies on which it was based: (1) being targeted to a specific population of individuals, and (2) being implemented by respected leaders of the community rather than outsiders. While the gay population in San Francisco in the 1980s and '90s had some awareness of HIV/AIDS through outside sources, it was the interpersonal relationships within the community that were ultimately most influential in changing behaviors and alleviating the HIV/AIDS epidemic in the city.

Study #3: Save the Children

In 1991, Jerry Sternin, a visiting scholar at Tufts University and the director of Save the Children in Vietnam, was asked to create an effective, large-scale program to combat child malnutrition in the region. At the time, more than 65 percent of all children living in Vietnamese villages were malnourished.

Utilizing a "positive deviance" model—an approach that focuses on identifying what is going right in order to amplify it, as opposed to focusing on what is going wrong in order to fix it—Sternin sought out poor families that had been able to avoid malnutrition without having access to special resources. These families were the "positive deviants"—*positive* because they were doing things right, and *deviants* because they engaged in behaviors that deviated from the norm. Sternin helped the community discover that mothers in these families collected tiny shrimps and crabs from paddy fields and added them, alongside sweet potato greens, to their children's meals. While these foods were accessible to everyone, most community members believed they were inappropriate for young children. Also, these mothers were feeding their children three to four times a day, rather than the customary two times a day.

Sternin helped the community members create a program that allowed them to emulate the behavior of these positive deviants. Mothers whose children were malnourished were asked to forage for shrimps, crabs, and sweet potato greens. Then, in the company of other mothers, they were taught to cook new recipes that their children ate. Within weeks, mothers could see their children becoming healthier. After the two-year pilot project, malnutrition had decreased by 85 percent in the communities where this approach was implemented. Over the next several years, this intervention became a nationwide program in Vietnam, helping over 500,000 children improve their nutritional status.

Positive deviance is an offshoot of the diffusion of innovations model in that it questions the role of outside expertise, believing that the wisdom to solve problems lies within communities and organizations. In the positive deviance approach, the role of outside experts is not to come in and make changes; it is to identify the uncommon and effective things that positive deviants do within their community and then make them visible and actionable. The role of the expert is mainly to facilitate a process that can help amplify local wisdom. In doing so, solutions and benefits can be sustained.

The positive deviance approach works because the community or organization owns the problem, as well as its solutions. Positive deviance has been used to address such diverse issues as combating childhood anemia, curbing the trafficking of young women, and increasing school retention rates. Keep this positive deviance model in mind throughout this book, especially as it relates to the role of your champions. While champions can serve a variety of functions, they can often be utilized to solve problems and find solutions in your organization at the local level, focusing on what is being done right (not just reporting on what is being done wrong) and finding ways to encourage and spread this positive behavior.

THE SOCIAL SCIENCE BEHIND
THE SPREAD OF IDEAS

Almost 100 years of diffusion research has taught us that the spread of ideas depends on interpersonal communication within social networks. There are three sociological concepts at play that support this diffusion research: social conformity, social proof, and social currency.

Social Conformity

People conform to the behaviors of those around them—everything from *"Where should we go on vacation?"* to *"Is this new policy or initiative worth supporting?"* We want people to think positively of us, so sometimes we go along with others to fit in and not be difficult. Ever have an opinion you failed to express in a meeting or among friends because you thought everyone else was against it? Or have you gone along with an opinion because it seemed the group was in favor of it, even though you may not have been? When other people are doing something, it can subtly cause you to think, *"I should be doing that, too."*

It's human nature to conform; those seeking to influence others are well-advised to use human nature to their advantage.

Social Proof

Closely related to the concept of social conformity is social proof. When trying to figure out what we should do or what ideas to adopt, we look to what is going on around us—not because we necessarily want to conform but because what's going on around us is the simplest way to obtain information. Good or bad, we use the behaviors and information that we see around us to inform our own judgment.

Social Currency

People share ideas to make themselves appear more knowledgeable. For example, if we talk about a new technology or the latest trend in our industry, people perceive us as having "insider status." The more we care about or value that idea, the more likely we are to pass it along—whether our goal is to look knowledgeable or to genuinely help others.

This concept is referred to as "social currency." We bring something of value (an idea) to others, and, in exchange, it elevates our social identity or worth.

MAINTAINING NETWORK PERSPECTIVE

Social networks play a critical role in spreading ideas across an organization. Strong connections within your network provide opportunities for people to access valuable information and resources they wouldn't have been able to access in isolation. The connections in your social network influence your ideas, attitudes, and behaviors.

The most powerful network connections are often informal. To put this concept into practice, you need to maintain *network perspective*: the ability to look beyond formal structures within an organization and see the complex, informal web of connections between people. The importance of these people in creating influence is often overlooked or underemphasized in organizations with a formal, hierarchical structure.

Your ideal champions may not be your CEO, VPs, and senior executives. In many cases, they may not be your middle-level management. Your champions should be trusted and influential colleagues at *all* levels of your organization. They're the people who can collaborate across organizational hierarchies, regions, departments, and demographics to influence others and spread ideas, regardless of their job titles or formal role within the organization. Complex challenges cannot be addressed by individuals alone, and rarely can they be addressed effectively in a top-down approach.

> Champions networks are not about hierarchy. They are built on the strength of network connections.

The concept of network perspective is key to everything discussed in this book. Champions networks are not about hierarchy. They are built on the strength of network connections. A successful champions network includes champions with strong connections who serve as catalysts for collaboration, influencing their colleagues and spreading ideas across their organization.

Armed with a better understanding of how ideas spread, you need to create a network to facilitate this spread of ideas and influence across your organization. While an idea can be shared in an email, a poster campaign, or a company-wide meeting, those only create initial awareness of the idea. To ensure that your idea is valued and spread across your organization, you need to create a network in which your ideas are *champion*ed. In doing so, your ideas won't just exist in your head, or in a policy, or in an email—they'll be *alive*.

Ready to expand your influence by learning how to build a champions network? First, let's look at what a champions network is and how it benefits your organization or community.

"If you want to bring fundamental change in people's beliefs and behavior, you need to create a community around them, where those new beliefs can be practiced and expressed and nurtured."

MALCOLM GLADWELL, JOURNALIST AND AUTHOR

2

WHAT IS A CHAMPIONS NETWORK?

Champions Network: *a group of individuals who aim to bring awareness, integration, or change to an organization relating to a matter they are not experts on but have been chosen to advocate for.*

Champions networks can be found across a range of industries and sectors, in the corporate world, government, academia, and philanthropy. Some champions networks draw from employees within an organization while others pull from outside resources. They comprise employees who represent and advocate for a breadth of organizational initiatives, issues, and ideas, ranging from compliance and ethics to corporate responsibility, cybersecurity, health and wellness, workplace safety, and employee recruitment. Champions can be utilized to introduce and adopt a new organizational process, program, way of working, or culture shift. Regardless of its structure or purpose, a champions network is meant to provide *continuous* support and engagement, with champions having multiple responsibilities to achieve an overall objective.

> Regardless of its structure or purpose, a champions network is meant to provide *continuous* support and engagement.

First, let's clear up one potential point of confusion: What does it mean to be a "champion?"

WHAT IS A "CHAMPION?"

The word *champion* is not used throughout this book in the more traditional context: a victor who has achieved status or recognition by conquering competitors.

Rather, champions are those who *champion* ideas, initiatives, or causes across an organization. While the word could be better described as an advocate or a guide in some organizations, the term *champions network* has become ubiquitous in the corporate world and other organizational contexts. So, we'll use it throughout this book with the understanding that it isn't the only way to describe this model. You may prefer or have come to use a different term with the same meaning attached to it—for example, the term *ambassadors network* has become a popular alternative.

The name itself is far less important than almost everything else discussed in this book. It may help to have a catchy name that complements your subject matter or your organization's brand, but the success of your champions network won't depend on what you call it.

I prefer the term *champions network* for two reasons. First, it's recognizable. Many professionals have seen the term before and may have a general understanding of what it entails. Second, the definition of a "champion" in this context is proactive: *a person who advocates for an issue, idea, or cause.* In other words, your champions aren't just representatives, they are proactive partners in your efforts.

WHAT SHOULD I CALL MY CHAMPIONS NETWORK?

Whatever name you choose for your network, here are a few points to consider:

Be Consistent

If there are three different types of "champions networks" within your organization that are well-known and well received, you may want to stick with that title. However, if you're trying to differentiate your network from other networks that have been less popular or successful, you may want to drop the "champions" moniker.

Keep It Simple

Try to avoid unnecessary layers or a multitude of different titles for your champions. In doing research for this book, I came across a company with a three-tiered champions network. Champions were given different titles (*advocate*, *focal*, and *guide*) depending on their responsibilities within the network. In general, this is an unnecessarily complex way to structure a champions network and a good way to confuse people within your organization.

Be Creative

If your organization is ACME Incorporated, the ACME Advocates might make for a catchy, alliterative name. Consider having an internal naming competition to gain some publicity for your network. Just don't get stuck on the word "champion" if it's not the right fit. I challenged myself to come up with a name for every letter of the alphabet (excluding the "C") to demonstrate the potential for creativity. (Warning: some of the names on the next page may be more acceptable than others; no need to offend anyone in designing your champions network.) Do any of the names on the next page sound good? Have better ideas? Jot them down here:

_____

_____

_____

_____

Ambassador: one who acts as a representative of a specified activity.

Backer: a person who supports someone or something.

Diplomat: an appointed representative of a government or department.

Escort: a person accompanying another for protection or as a mark of rank.

Focal: relating to the center or main point of interest.

Guide: a person who advises or shows the way to others.

Helper: a person who helps someone else.

Insider: a person within a group who is privy to information unavailable to others.

Joiner: a person who readily joins groups or campaigns.

King: a man who holds a preeminent position.

Leader: a person who commands a group or organization.

Mouthpiece: one who expresses or interprets another's views.

Networker: one who interacts or exchanges information with others.

Officer: one who holds an office of trust, authority, or command.

Proponent: one who argues in favor of something.

Queen: a woman who holds a preeminent position.

Representative: one who represents another, invested with authority.

Supporter: a person who approves of and encourages someone or something.

Torchbearer: someone in the forefront of a campaign, crusade, or movement.

Usher: a person who shows or guides someone.

Vanguard: a person leading the way in new developments or ideas.

Watcher: a person who closely follows or observes someone or something.

X Factor: a person who has a strong but unpredictable influence.

Yeoman: a person attending or assisting another.

Zealot: a person who is fanatical and uncompromising in pursuit of their ideals.

THE ROLE OF A CHAMPION

Champions can be recruited across geographic regions, sites, or departments to help advocate for the widespread adoption of an idea, program, or initiative within an organization. Champions generally operate at a local level, so they are well-situated to spread ideas and influence; because champions know their departments, sites, and colleagues well, they can have a greater impact on messaging and awareness than a centralized function, which is farther removed from localized operations.

Below is a list to keep in mind pertaining to what a champion *is* and what a champion is *not*. Many of the bullet points below will be discussed in depth and in greater context in this book.

A Champion Is:

- An employee with full-time responsibilities other than their champion role.
- A well-respected and trusted individual among their peers.
- A representative of a belief, practice, program, or policy.
- A facilitator of dialogue and a catalyst for collaboration.
- The local eyes and ears within an organization.
- A proactive partner with leaders in your network and broader organization.
- An advocate for ideas, issues, and initiatives that need to be spread.
- Visible and accessible to management and colleagues.
- A role model for company values and behavior.
- An information gatherer and provider.
- When necessary, someone who escalates issues or questions to experts.

A Champion Is Not:

- A subject-matter expert in the area they champion.
- Paid extra to serve in the role (however, some incentives may be offered).

- Someone who does other peoples' work for them.
- Appointed as a punishment for poor performance.
- A champion in perpetuity (champions' roles are limited in time).

THE MOTIVATION OF A CHAMPION

Champions serve for a variety of reasons. Even if they are assigned to the role, they usually have some motivation (personal or organizational) for agreeing to serve as a champion.

Personal Motivations

A champion may have a personal connection to promoting a certain issue or cause. For example, their interest in serving as a Health and Wellness Champion may stem from overcoming their own health struggles, or their desire to serve as a Privacy Champion may be directly related to an instance where their online identity was stolen. Champions may also have a greater altruistic purpose in serving in the role, such as promoting environmental sustainability. Many champions serve because they have a genuine interest in and enjoy solving problems and achieving the sense of accomplishment that comes with the job.

Organizational Motivations

A champion may see a need to have their organization recognized as one that cares about an issue or cause as part of its brand identity—for example, a company with a strong ethical culture or one that encourages philanthropic work. Some champions have a desire to ensure that their personal values and goals align with those of their organizational culture. Other champions may have less of an altruistic purpose for serving—they hope to achieve professional recognition from their management or peers by serving in the role.

CHALLENGES FACED BY CHAMPIONS

The role of a champion comes with its challenges; below are a few examples. The following chapters will address some of these concerns and how they can be mitigated.

Negative Perceptions from Colleagues

Some champions may be perceived as "spies" by their colleagues, assigned to look for bad behavior to report to management. Other colleagues may see champions as taking away some of *their* current responsibilities—people don't mind support in their job role, but in general, they don't appreciate it when their "power" (real or perceived) is taken away from them.

Tension between Priorities

Sometimes the priority of a champion in advocating for an idea or initiative is at odds with other business priorities. For example, many good ideas bring with them a greater financial commitment to the organization or a strain on employees' time. Champions are required to balance these competing priorities and must be able to explain how their ideas can help to *support* business priorities, rather than compete with them.

Lack of Evaluation Metrics

Some of the concepts and ideas that a champion may be asked to advocate for can be difficult to measure—for example: compliance and ethics, health and wellness, and corporate social responsibility. Leadership can be hesitant and champions may face pushback when the benefits of a champions network can't be clearly measured.

Technical Complexity

While champions aren't expected to be experts on the ideas they advocate for, they do need to have a basic knowledge of concepts that can often be complex to understand and implement (e.g., international sanctions compliance, risk management, or cybersecurity initiatives). A big part of being a champion is learning how to translate complex ideas and requirements into language that can be understood and adopted by the wider workforce.

THE BENEFITS OF A CHAMPIONS NETWORK

With a better understanding of what a champions network is (and what it isn't), the roles of champions, and their motivations and challenges, we can turn to answering the most important question: *Why* build a champions network in your organization?

Promote Your Big Ideas

A champions network is an ideal way to build awareness and support for your ideas, regardless of the form they take. As discussed previously, the best way to influence others is to find those early adopters and influencers who can help spread and support your ideas. These are your champions!

Address Gaps in Head Count

If you don't have the budget to hire a full-time professional, adding champions can help to supplement these gaps at a relatively low cost to the organization.

Be Your Eyes and Ears

Champions can be trained to spot and report local issues, concerns, or developments that may otherwise go unnoticed by a centralized department.

Educate Your Colleagues

Champions networks can bring individuals into an area to which they ordinarily would have limited access. As a result, your champions will gain greater knowledge in a new area, as well as a greater appreciation for the job you do every day.

Show Initiative

Developing a champions network to address gaps and support organizational initiatives shows your commitment to your company and its continued success.

Be a Part of Something Bigger

Consider using a champions network to make your individual role a larger function by creating a team of champions who work with you to carry out your objectives.

Accomplish Corrective Actions

Champions networks can serve as a formal corrective action to address gaps or vulnerabilities that have been identified as the result of an internal audit.

Support Company Culture

Champions networks can be used to help create a new company culture or enforce an existing culture, including its shared values, attitudes, goals, and practices.

Increase Employee Retention

Employees stay longer when they feel involved and when their expertise is valued. A champions network is a great way to create and sustain employee involvement.

Create Social Connection

Champions networks can help foster increased social connection and promote a collaborative workplace environment. This is especially true post-COVID, with the work-from-home model becoming the new normal for many organizations.

Set the Tone at the Middle

It's not as popular a phrase as "tone at the top," but champions can often be more effective than the C-suite in modeling organizational behaviors and standards.

Facilitate Communication

At their core, champions networks are a platform through which communication can be facilitated and strengthened within an organization. An increase in communication leads to an increased sense of transparency and trust among the wider workforce.

Identify Business Challenges and Solutions

Champions don't just spot problems, they find solutions. Train your champions to be proactive partners, and their support in implementing solutions will be invaluable.

Connect the Central to the Local

Champions networks bring your organization together by connecting a centralized function to sites and people that might otherwise feel removed from the company.

Share Stories

The best way to learn from others and increase engagement in a company is through stories. "We tried initiative 'X' and it worked, we tried program 'Y' and it failed." Champions networks create a platform for organizational storytelling to thrive.

Offer Professional Development Opportunities

Do you have an employee who is looking for added responsibility or an opportunity to develop their skill sets? Being a champion offers development opportunities without costly financial investments.

Create Organizational Distinction

Is your organization looking to stand out in its field? The implementation of a well-run champions network can help to build a company's brand and reputation.

Now that you understand what a champions network is, the psychology behind it, the research that supports it, and the benefits it can bring, let's put theory into practice. The following section provides your blueprint to build a successful champions network.

PART II

THE BLUEPRINT

"The secret of getting ahead is getting started. The secret of getting started is breaking your complex overwhelming tasks into small manageable tasks, and starting on the first one."

MARK TWAIN, AMERICAN WRITER

3

GAINING LEADERSHIP COMMITMENT

The first step in building any champions network is gaining commitment from your leadership. Exactly what this support looks like and who needs to provide it may differ from one organization to the next. Because champions networks can involve multiple sites, departments, and disciplines, the necessary leadership buy-in may extend in multiple directions, across different segments of the organization. Be prepared to ask for buy-in from different levels and different departments, and to tailor your message to them. A one-time pitch or a one-size-fits-all approach to gaining buy-in may not be enough, depending on the type of network you plan to operate and the size of your organization.

For example, your champions network may have been approved by *your* direct supervisor, but have you gained the support of leaders who manage your champions? Remember, you're asking champions to devote some part of their job role to taking on new tasks, so you should expect pushback (or at least a few questions) from your champions' supervisors and other leaders within the organization.

Gaining this initial buy-in is critical—if you don't have the support of leadership throughout the development and implementation process, your champions network is destined to fail. The best way to earn this buy-in is by creating an organized network structure ahead of time so management and leadership know what to expect. It's at this initial stage where your momentum for the champions network begins to build, so take advantage of the opportunity. Let's take a closer look at exactly why leadership buy-in is so crucial and how to achieve it.

WHY GET COMMITMENT AHEAD OF TIME?

Gaining buy-in and support from your senior leadership prior to the implementation of a champions network is crucial to its success. I learned this lesson the hard way at a prior company where I worked.

When I was brought into that company to start a champions network, I assumed that the management buy-in was already there. I had been told that the internal audit function had recommended that my specific department (Trade Compliance) set up a champions network to help address compliance gaps. This recommendation was made, in part, because the organization already had several champions networks (privacy, ethics, and cybersecurity). To the best of my knowledge, these networks were perceived favorably and were operating effectively. Therefore, I skipped the first step of gaining leadership buy-in. I started structuring the network and recruiting without so much as speaking to anyone at the leadership level of the organization.

> Gaining buy-in and support from your senior leadership prior to the implementation of a champions network is crucial to its success.

What I came to understand later was that leadership was not aware of this recommendation nor had they been told that I was hired to develop such a network. Another life lesson learned the hard way: don't assume that everyone knows who you are and what you have been hired to accomplish. It was only later, after I had begun the process of recruitment and program development in earnest, that management and senior leadership started to come to me with questions like: *"Who approved this initiative?"* As it turned out, no one had.

As a result of not getting the necessary buy-in ahead of time, I found myself doing a lot of justifying and explaining the network to leaders within my organization—many of whom were not easily sold on the concept of a trade-compliance champions network. While this is a necessary step in the process, it's preferably done *before* you've already put in so much work.

In addition to receiving buy-in from the executive leadership in your organization, you should be looking to gain buy-in from mid-level management within all the departments from which you intend to recruit your champions. Asking an employee to take on additional responsibility as a champion takes away from their day-to-day job roles. This can, understandably, be poorly received by some managers and department heads. It's your job as the leader of the network to make clear to leadership the added value that the network brings. Ensure that management is aware of the planned implementation of the champions network *and* encourage company leaders and managers to provide input before, during, and after the implementation process.

Below are just a few reasons why getting management's buy-in and support ahead of time is crucial to a successful champions network:

- Receiving management's input and advice early in the process helps you develop a better champions network in the long run.
- Management "owns" the resources (your champions) and therefore should be a partner in the success of your network.
- Addressing pushback and criticism ahead of time saves you a lot of headaches and backtracking down the road.
- Even if they are hesitant or have questions, management appreciates being asked to provide input. Your willingness to take their input helps to garner their support in the development of your network.
- Management may help you secure a budget to operate the network.

DEVELOP AN IMPLEMENTATION PLAN

The most effective way to gain management buy-in and support for your champions network is to create a formal implementation plan. Creating a plan serves several purposes. First, a formal plan allows you to clarify in your own mind the purpose and structure of your champions network—if *you* don't understand why a champions network is needed and what is entailed in its implementation, no one else will. Second, having a formal plan allows you to better communicate with your leadership the purpose of your network and shows that you have taken the time to define a structure. Of course, your formal plan and the eventual structure of your network may take on many iterations, based on input you receive from leadership. Your plan can be used throughout the development of your champions network to keep you organized and on target as you work toward implementation.

In your plan, provide a structure for the network that will clearly demonstrate what the champions network is (and what it is not), what is expected from champions, and the value that the network brings to the organization. Include a timeline so management and internal stakeholders see when to expect the completion of certain milestones. Providing a clear structure also shows that your network is a well-organized initiative and demonstrates your commitment to its success.

Topics within the implementation plan may include any of those listed below. (This list tracks closely with the content in Chapters 4 through 8 of this book.)

The Structure of the Network
- Purpose of the network (compliance, security, wellness, recruitment, etc.).
- Organization of the network (regions, sites, departments, etc.).
- Size of the network and number of champions.
- Defined roles and responsibilities of champions.

Recruiting Champions
- How champions are recruited to serve.
- What potential incentives may be offered.
- Who qualifies to serve in the champion's role.
- How many champions per region, department, or site.

Training Champions
- Training schedule for champions.
- Elements of a training program.
- Summary of the substantive training (e.g., understanding anti-bribery law).
- Summary of the non-substantive training topics (e.g., communication skills).

Network Implementation
- Avenues for internal communication within the network.
- Plans to respond to challenges that arise.
- How the network will be publicized across the organization.
- Strategies to keep champions engaged and active.

Demonstrating Network Success
- Metrics to be used to demonstrate network success.
- Developments to be shared with organizational leaders.
- Strategies to benchmark against other champions networks.
- Plans for continued network growth and improvement.

GIVE A PRESENTATION TO LEADERSHIP

Using the plan you have prepared, provide a formal presentation to your C-suite, senior executives, or any other level of management from which you'll need commitment. Try to get time during a board of directors meeting if you can. As well as outlining what is already in your written plan, be sure to emphasize and demonstrate the need for a champions network at your organization, which can be done by showing:

- Organizational vulnerabilities or gaps resolved by a champions network.
- How a champions network helps address a specific organizational concern.
- Examples of successful champions networks in your organization or industry.
- Added value and business benefits of the network to your organization.

During your presentation, offer the opportunity for leaders to be directly involved in the network by serving as "leadership champions." They may not provide as much day-to-day support as other champions, but their involvement creates more accountability and visible leadership approval for the network.

During or after your presentation, be prepared to respond to the tough questions and pushback you'll receive from leadership. You may find that this resistance helps you develop a stronger program. Here are examples of pushback you may receive from leadership, followed by ways to respond.

"My employees aren't responsible for this."

The simplest response here is: *"Everyone is responsible."* It's difficult for leadership to argue that everyone in your organization isn't responsible in some respects for areas like compliance, safety, or cybersecurity (just to name a few).

"My employees shouldn't be doing the work of subject-matter experts."

Your champions are *never* the subject-matter experts. This should be made clear in your formal proposal and presentation to leadership. While you are asking champions to maintain a higher level of knowledge than most employees about certain areas and to be prepared to support a core function, champions are never meant to take the place of subject-matter experts within the organization.

"My employees don't have time to take on any extra work."

Management should understand that the role of a champion is limited in its scope and time commitment. Champions are asked to serve for a limited time (usually a year or two) with a designated percentage of time allotted for a champion's work. For example, a champion's responsibilities may only require attending formal meetings for an hour every quarter while remaining available for individual tasks as they arise. So, make it clear to a champion's manager that their role will not pull them away from their day-to-day duties for an unreasonable or extended period.

That being said, depending on your network and how much you are asking of your champions, an employee may very well not have a free minute in their day to take on champion responsibilities. If this is the case, ask a manager if there is another person on his team or within her region or department who could fulfill the champions role. The last thing you want is to have champions in your network who serve grudgingly or who can't devote adequate time to their new role.

Gaining leadership approval and support is a crucial first step in the development of your champions network. However, if you continue to face resistance (or have your own uncertainties) about implementing a champions network, consider starting a pilot program—a small number of champions covering a limited number of sites or departments. Success with a pilot program may provide the momentum and evidence needed to eventually develop a larger, longer-term network. A limited pilot program may also help you identify issues and make necessary adjustments on a smaller level before eventually scaling up the network.

Next, let's look at creating your network structure.

"Walking on water is easy if you know where to step."

PETER TIERYAS, KOREAN AMERICAN WRITER

4

CREATING THE NETWORK STRUCTURE

Creating a formal structure for your champions network achieves multiple goals. You establish legitimacy for your network if you have an organized structure with clear documentation and accountability for all network participants. A formal structure clarifies the responsibilities of champions so they know what to expect of the program and what is expected of them. Finally, a formal structure helps you, the network leader, stay organized and on target.

The layout and reporting structure of your network will vary depending on its size. For example, a network of five to twenty champions may all report back directly to the champions network leader (the subject-matter expert), whereas a network of twenty or more champions that spans multiple regions, sites, and departments may require subsets of reporting structures to keep the network manageable and organized.

On the following pages are two examples of champions network structures. These are general templates; your specific network will vary in layout and reporting structure. Also, while these are relatively simplistic structures from a bird's-eye view, between each layer there is information cascading down, communications happening in all directions, and reporting from the bottom to the top, all of which make for an intricate champions network once it is fully implemented and operational.

THE STRUCTURE OF A SMALL CHAMPIONS NETWORK

The **champions network leader** (a subject-matter expert) oversees recruiting, training, and communicating directly with every **champion**. Each **champion** is embedded in a different department of the organization. Each **champion** is tasked with carrying out his or her responsibilities and reporting back to the **champions network leader**. In turn, the **champions network leader** may report back to a department head, a senior leader, or a C-suite executive.

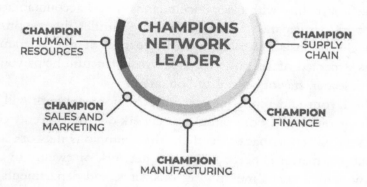

THE STRUCTURE OF A MEDIUM/LARGE CHAMPIONS NETWORK

The **champions network leader** (a subject-matter expert) may only be responsible for recruiting, training, and communicating directly with each **head champion**, who in turn recruits, trains, and communicates directly with each individual **champion** in his or her department. A **head champion** is not a subject-matter expert; however, he or she likely has leadership experience. Each individual **champion** reports back to a **head champion**, who in turn reports back to the **champions network leader**. The larger the network grows, the more sublevels may be necessary to keep it manageable. A network that is very large (100+ champions) may require additional subject-matter experts to be brought in to oversee regional or departmental subgroups to ensure that the network remains manageable in its recruiting, training, communication, and reporting functions.

Regardless of how your champions network is structured from an organizational and reporting standpoint, all network structures need to include the following four aspects: the purpose, the scope, network leader responsibilities, and champion responsibilities. These four essential components provide those in the network *and* those outside the network with an understanding of what the champions network is and how it operates.

Consider putting all four of these pieces into a single document—a *Champions Network Charter*—that is made available to organizational leadership, all champions, and anyone in your organization who is looking to understand the nature and operation of the network. This transparency helps you and your champions stay on target and remain accountable in your roles.

THE PURPOSE

The purpose of your champions network is unique to you and your organization. As discussed in the previous chapters, the goals of a champions network can vary widely. Regardless of what your purpose is, it needs to be stated succinctly in your network charter. For example, a purpose statement for a cybersecurity champions network could be written as follows:

Purpose

To utilize knowledgeable local employees as part-time advocates for cybersecurity initiatives throughout the organization, helping to:

- ✓ Create employee engagement.
- ✓ Increase the culture of cybersecurity.
- ✓ Create a greater organizational awareness of cybersecurity.
- ✓ Spread programs and initiatives across their designated site or department.

That template can be easily adapted to almost any subject matter and can be adjusted depending on the overall goals of your network. The purpose statement is a chance to clearly state the goals of the network and the role of the champions in helping to achieve them. Ideally, these goals will align with broader organizational goals or values.

THE SCOPE

Your network charter needs to clearly state the anticipated scope of your network. Scope refers to where your champions will be located, how many champions there will be, and how the champions will be organized (e.g., by department or region).

Ideally, you may want a champion in every major geographic region, department, business unit, and site. However, it may make more sense to launch your network within a limited scope and then scale up as needed.

Employee population density is only one factor to consider in determining where to locate champions—i.e., don't just put the most champions where the most employees are located. Carefully consider *why* champions need to be more concentrated in certain regions or departments. For example, some geographic areas may be more susceptible to corruption concerns, while other regions or sites may have a higher instance of workplace safety concerns. Depending on the type of network you are developing, there are numerous factors to consider when determining where and how many champions to assign to a location.

> As the leader of your champions network, you'll have several roles to play in its management and operation.

NETWORK LEADER RESPONSIBILITIES

As the leader of your champions network, you'll have several roles to play in its management and operation. Be sure to include a section that outlines these key responsibilities in your network charter, including:

- Obtaining initial and continued support from organizational leadership.
- Determining realistic and reasonable responsibilities for champions and continuing to remind champions of them.
- Defining the purpose and objectives of the network.
- Recruiting the champions.
- Implementing an initial training program and schedule for all champions.
- Holding monthly/quarterly meetings with champions.
- Meeting periodically with individual champions to discuss specific matters.
- Communicating with champions to provide updates, disseminate new information, and inquire about local developments or concerns.
- Monitoring the program, looking for gaps and needed improvements.
- Publicizing the network and its champions throughout the organization.
- Staying up to date on regulatory changes, new organizational policies, or external developments of which champions should be informed.
- Remaining open to feedback and constructive criticism from champions concerning the operation of the network.
- Establishing metrics to demonstrate network success.
- Reporting network updates (good and bad) to organizational leadership.
- Addressing issues, questions, and concerns that are escalated by champions.
- Recognizing the individual accomplishments of champions and their continued commitment to their roles.

CHAMPION RESPONSIBILITIES

Your champions will likely be asked to take on several responsibilities. Outlining these responsibilities in your network charter is the first step to ensure there is clarity among your champions as to what is expected from them. Responsibilities should always be reasonable and achievable. The list below provides a good sampling of the types of roles and responsibilities your champions may be asked to take on:

- Act as a trusted person and point of contact to whom local employees can go.
- Promote awareness and engagement at the local or departmental level.
- Assist the network leader in disseminating policies and communications.
- Showcase the desired behaviors that other employees are encouraged to adopt.
- Assist in the coordination and execution of local investigations, as needed.
- Be proactive in spotting issues and concerns at the local level.
- Make time when approached by employees with questions.
- Maintain confidentiality regarding potential violations of internal policy.
- Participate in training and meetings conducted by the network leader.
- Communicate in a timely and transparent manner with the network leader.
- Provide feedback to the network leader regarding what is working well and what is not.
- Escalate serious issues to the network leader or another subject-matter expert.

Annual Performance Plan

In addition to including these responsibilities in the charter, network leaders should also consider consulting with Human Resources and a champion's manager about including some (or all) of these responsibilities in the champion's annual performance plan. Generally, such plans designate a certain percentage of time that an employee is expected to devote to a project or goal for the year. Including a realistic percentage of time that the employee is expected to devote to the champion's role (no matter how small the percentage) within a performance plan formalizes the employee's new role as a champion and increases accountability.

With support from your organization's leadership and a structure in place, you can begin the next critical step in building your network: recruiting your champions.

"Fight for the things that you care about but do it in a way that will lead others to join you."

RUTH BADER GINSBURG, U.S. SUPREME COURT JUSTICE

5

RECRUITING THE CHAMPIONS

If you want to build a champions network, you're going to need champions! Employees who have developed trust among their colleagues and who know their organization often make excellent champions. While not a requirement, employees with an interest or background in the substantive area of the network can be valuable. However, successful champions networks often include employees with varying levels of expertise and experience. There is no single mold that every champion should fit. Most importantly, you are looking for *willing* volunteers who have an interest in filling the champions role.

The guidance that follows is for networks that are actively recruiting champions. When starting a champions network, it may make sense initially to recruit champions and then switch to an application process once the program is more established.

HOW TO FIND THE RIGHT CHAMPIONS

The first step in recruiting champions is to make your organization aware of your champions network and the recruitment process. How you position and announce the network can have a big impact on its ultimate success. Consider having the initial announcement come from as high up as your CEO or another C-suite representative, and make it clear in the announcement that senior leadership supports the implementation of the network.

Avenues of Recruitment

There are many ways to recruit champions, including:

- Advertising the champions network and champions role in intra-company newsletters, postings, social media channels, and emails.
- Taking five minutes at the end of employee training sessions (compliance training, cybersecurity training, safety training, etc.) to talk about the applicable champions network and to recruit volunteers.
- Setting up table tents in communal areas of the office to advertise the network.
- Initiating a poster campaign or taking a more modern (and economical) approach by posting electronic advertisements on LCD screens in the office.
- Asking colleagues, company leaders, Human Resources representatives, and local managers to nominate promising individuals.
- Using technology to your advantage by initiating a virtual recruitment campaign via internal instant messaging platforms that your organization utilizes (e.g., Slack or Yammer).
- Asking your HR department if you can present your champions network to new hires at an onboarding meeting.
- Asking your internal communications team how to best get your message across to a wide but targeted audience.
- Holding a lunchtime event or joining another organizational event to help publicize the network and attract potential champions.
- Asking colleagues to promote the network at meetings and team briefings.

The broader and more creative you get in recruiting champions, the more likely you are to attract employees that truly represent a cross section of your organization. Try to avoid relying *only* on electronic means to promote your network, as some employees (e.g., manufacturing) may not have regular access to a computer.

One of the strategies I found to be effective in recruiting champions is to write a short article, post it on my company's intranet site, and then wait to see who leaves a comment. The article doesn't necessarily have to be about the champions network itself, but it can be related to the substantive area of the network.

For example, if you are recruiting for a trade-compliance champions network, write an article about recent geopolitical developments that may be impacting your organization. See who leaves a comment (positive or negative) in reaction to the article, and

> Ideally, you are looking for a diverse array of champions that represent a cross section of your organization.

then respond accordingly: *"Looks like you have a real interest in this topic, would you be interested in speaking with me about serving as a trade-compliance champion?"*

Cast a Wide Net

Your search for champions should be relatively broad. Ideally, you are looking for a diverse array of champions that represent a cross section of your organization. Diversity can take many forms. In addition to looking for candidates across geographic regions, sites, business units, and departments, look for candidates with different titles and seniority levels. Remember, those who are considered the most trusted and influential among their colleagues are not necessarily those with the fanciest titles or biggest offices.

A diverse pool of champions also includes different cultures, languages, ethnicities, and genders. After all, the more diverse your champions, the more likely your messages and ideas will be to reach a broader and more diverse array of employees across the organization.

THE CRITERIA FOR A CHAMPION

While there is no single mold that every champion needs to fit, in your recruiting process you should be looking for certain qualities that tend to make more effective champions. Whether they are identified by managers or evaluated through your interview process (as described later in this chapter), keep the following characteristics in mind as you search for the right champions for your network:

- Respected, trusted, and well-connected among their peers.
- Able to effectively build coalitions and influence others' behavior.
- Familiar with or have an interest in the subject matter of the network.
- Knowledgeable about the overall organization, including its operation.
- Familiar with their local or departmental culture, practices, and issues.
- Practical problem solvers who look to facilitate and resolve conflicts.
- Enthusiastic, with a high degree of engagement and responsiveness.
- Approachable, with good listening and communications skills.
- A willing volunteer, available to commit the needed time and effort to the role.
- Able to clearly communicate complex ideas.

INTERVIEWING POTENTIAL CHAMPIONS

When recruiting champions, consider asking each candidate to go through an interview process. During the interview, you are looking to evaluate the candidate's:

- Relevant qualities and characteristics (see previous section).
- Overall interest in the role.

- Ability to commit the time required.
- Willingness to complete the required tasks and responsibilities.

Here are a few questions to ask potential champions to evaluate their fit for the role:

"Why are you interested in this role?"
"How have you successfully influenced people in the past?"
"What skills do you think you'd bring to the position?"
"What example can you give of a time when you have solved a conflict?"
"What example can you give of a project you completed end to end?"
"What work accomplishment are you most proud of?"
"What do you think are the best ways to motivate people?"
"How will you make time for this additional responsibility?"

THE JOB DESCRIPTION AND APPOINTMENT LETTER

Consider providing all potential champions and their managers with a formal job description. The job description summarizes the main tasks of the champion, the characteristics that make for a successful champion, and any additional information that may be relevant. Once the candidate has been chosen, formally appoint them to the role via a letter that restates the information provided in the job description. The appointment letter should be signed by (1) the network leader, (2) someone in a senior leadership position, (3) the champion, and (4) the champion's manager. This serves as formal recognition of the role's responsibilities and time commitment. Providing this type of documentation adds a sense of legitimacy to your network. The job description and appointment letter also clarify for champions and their manager what is expected in the role. On the following pages are a template job description and appointment letter that are easily adapted to almost any type of champions network.

Job Description: [NETWORK NAME] Champion

Champions serve as representatives and advocates for [SUBSTANTIVE AREA] as a first point of contact for employees in their designated region or department.

Main Tasks

- Act as a trusted person and neutral first point of contact whom local employees can look to for assistance.
- Escalate questions or concerns to experts.
- Promote [SUBSTANTIVE AREA] at the local level.
- Assist in the local dissemination of communications and policies.
- Provide support in local investigations, as required.
- Be proactive in spotting and reporting potential concerns.
- Make time to assist colleagues or ensure that they are directed to someone who can assist.
- Maintain confidentiality regarding legal or policy violations.
- Participate in network trainings and meetings.
- Communicate in a timely manner with the network leader.

Competencies and Characteristics

- Interest in [SUBSTANTIVE AREA] or willingness to learn.
- Willing to listen to employees' questions and concerns.
- Good written and verbal communication skills.
- Comfortable speaking with and motivating employees.
- Driven to seek organizational and process improvements.
- Proactive and task-oriented.
- Well-respected and trusted among colleagues.
- Willing to network across one's region, site, or department.
- Able to analyze details and communicate them effectively.
- Good at solving problems.
- Willing to be trained and receive constructive feedback.

Additional information

- Time commitment: [PERCENTAGE OR NUMBER OF HOURS].
- Champions are formally appointed by the network leader with the approval of the champion's manager.
- Appointments remain in effect for [LENGTH OF APPOINTMENT].

[DATE]

RE: [NAME OF NETWORK] **Appointment Letter**

Dear [EMPLOYEE NAME],

I am pleased to inform you of your appointment as [NETWORK NAME] Champion, representing [REGION OR DEPARTMENT]. In your role as a champion, you will:

- Act as a trusted person and neutral first point of contact whom local employees can turn to for assistance with questions or concerns.
- Escalate local questions or concerns that require the attention of experts.
- Promote local or departmental awareness of [SUBSTANTIVE AREA].
- Assist in the local dissemination of communications, policies, and guidance.
- Support the execution and coordination of local investigations, as required.
- Be proactive in spotting potential concerns and reporting them, as required.
- Make time to assist colleagues. If unable to make time or answer questions, ensure that employees are directed to someone who can assist.
- Maintain confidentiality regarding potential violations of internal policy.
- Participate in training/meetings organized by the Champions Network Leader.
- Communicate in a timely and transparent manner with the Champions Network Leader.

As the [NETWORK NAME] Leader and on behalf of [ORGANIZATION NAME], I thank you for accepting the champion role. Your signature and the signature of your manager below establish your acceptance and understanding of the champion role, its responsibilities, and its time commitment. For more information, or if you have any questions, please do not hesitate to reach out to me directly. In the meantime, please sign and return this letter once you and your manager have had an opportunity to discuss and agree on your appointment.

Sincerely,

[NAME AND SIGNATURE OF CHAMPIONS NETWORK LEADER]
[NAME AND SIGNATURE OF CHIEF/SENIOR EXECUTIVE]
[NAME AND SIGNATURE OF CHAMPION]
[NAME AND SIGNATURE OF CHAMPION'S MANAGER]

What do you do if you have *too many* people willing to serve as champions?

Be open to assigning certain champions on a rotating basis or as alternates who can fill in temporarily and eventually take the place of exiting champions. In general, try not to be so rigid in filling site or department quotas that you turn down willing participants who you believe would perform well in the role.

Now that you have recruited your champions, it's time to train them.

"Training is a process, not an event. It begins long before participants show up and continues until we see results in the workplace."

BOB PIKE, TRAINING PROFESSIONAL AND AUTHOR

6

TRAINING THE CHAMPIONS

Training is an opportunity to excite, engage, and educate your champions, not just on their responsibilities but how to effectively carry out those responsibilities. Training programs can be tailored to your specific champions network size, structure, and substance; however, almost all such training should share some commonalities.

Consider inviting a senior leader or C-suite executive to your initial training session to speak. This lends further credibility to your champions network and immediately lets your champions know they are visible and valued within the organization. Be sure to take time at the beginning of your training sessions to allow each champion to introduce themselves and explain why they have chosen to be a part of your champions network. Consider incorporating a team building or "getting to know you" activity as part of the initial training program for your champions.

On the following pages is an outline to use in developing effective training for your champions network. Whether your training is done in person or virtually, spread out over the course of a month, a week, or just a day, your training program should include several forms of knowledge and skill sets that can be broken down into four main categories: the substance, the context, the instruction, and the soft skills.

THE FOUR ELEMENTS OF A CHAMPIONS TRAINING PROGRAM

The Substance

While champions need not be subject-matter experts, they should receive some training on the substantive area of the champions network in which they serve. Some champions already have experience or a background in health and wellness, compliance and ethics, workplace safety, employee recruitment, sales, or any number of other areas. Other champions may have limited knowledge and experience, or none at all. Devote time in your training program to covering the substance that you want and expect your champions to understand.

In later chapters of this book, we'll look at four specific types of champions networks, including examples of the substance that may be the focus of their training programs. Your champions may not become experts, but you can provide enough requisite information about the subject matter to ensure they are knowledgeable.

The Context

Why does this champions network exist? This is one of the first questions to answer in the course of your training program. Even if your champions know or have come to learn about the substantive area, they should also understand why it's necessary to develop a champions network around this topic. What kinds of ideas, policies, guidelines, or awareness are the champions trying to spread or gain support for, and how do they help to achieve these objectives? This portion of your training makes clear what a successful champions network looks like, the benefits it brings, and its end

> A deeper understanding of the psychology behind the champions network model helps your champions better understand their role and greater purpose in the network.

goals. In other words, take time in your training program to help your champions understand *why* the network exists and *why* they have been chosen as champions.

During this part of your training, incorporate some of the research and psychology that was discussed in the first chapter of this book. While your champions may not need a detailed lecture on the diffusion of innovations, it may be helpful for them to understand why a champions network is an ideal way to spread ideas. A deeper understanding of the psychology behind the champions network model helps your champions better understand their role and greater purpose in the network.

The Instruction

This is the heart of your training program, where champions get the opportunity to understand how the network operates and what is expected of them in their role. Numerous forms of guidance can be provided during this instructional session, although most training tends to focus on the following points and information in one form or another:

- *Network policies, principles, and plans.*

These are organized in a formal network charter or other documentation.

- *The roles and responsibilities of champions.*

An extended explanation of those responsibilities stated in the job description.

- *The champions' authority and the limitations on such authority.*

For example, some champions are given the authority to conduct initial fact-finding missions at the local level while being prohibited from taking part in more consequential and sensitive investigations of a legal nature.

- *Reporting and communication channels.*

Champions are encouraged to communicate via email, phone, or other internal platforms at varying frequencies (weekly, monthly, quarterly).

- *Resources available to champions.*

These include intranet sites, company handbooks, internal policies, and other resources champions can refer to for information, both substantive and instructional.

- *Guidance for engaging with their colleagues.*

Champions are provided with creative ideas to spread awareness about a new program, initiative, or policy at the local level. Such ideas include brown-bag lunch sessions, a poster campaign, and virtual networking opportunities.

- *An explanation of the symbiotic nature of the champion role.*

Champions may be tasked by their network leaders to disseminate information, answer questions, and create local engagement and awareness. They also serve to keep the network leader aware of developments at the local level and work to proactively resolve local issues that might have otherwise gone unnoticed or unresolved if left solely to a centralized function.

The Soft Skills

A big part of the champion's role is working with people. Your training program may need to include some instruction on interpersonal skills—sometimes referred to as "soft skills"—that are necessary to be an effective champion. For example:

- Listening
- Coaching

- Communicating
- Networking
- Team building
- Brainstorming
- Problem-solving

If you have the budget for it, it may be worthwhile to bring in an outside expert or speaker to talk about any of the above topics. At the very least, the simplest way to train people on better interpersonal skills is to remind them to practice the golden rule; treating others how you want to be treated is, in general, the most effective way to get through to people and bring them to your side.

> *"The irony of 'soft skills' is that they're often the hardest to master."*
>
> **Adam Grant**, Organizational Psychologist and Author

HOW TO INFLUENCE YOUR CHAMPIONS

How can you, the network leader, influence your champions to remain engaged and active? In the early 1980s, researchers David Kipnis, Stuart Schmidt, and Ian Wilkinson studied the process of influence by measuring the frequency with which people in an organization used specific influencing tactics. Referred to as the *Profile of Organizational Influence Strategies* (POIS), this social science research is still used today by those wanting to better understand the types and success of influence tactics in organizations. The nine POIS influence strategies are defined on the following pages, along with explanations of how they can be utilized in the context of a champions network.

The Nine Influence Strategies

STRATEGY #1 - Requesting

Using orders, demands, or persistent reminders to influence others to act. This is often effective when the person giving the order is an authority figure.

For a straightforward or urgent task that needs to be done, this strategy may be the most effective and efficient in the context of a champions network. The network leader should request that champions attend required quarterly meetings, communicate policies and procedures in a timely manner, and report violations of company policy or law, all without the need to further justify or rationalize such requests.

STRATEGY #2 - Legitimating

Seeking to establish the legitimacy or rationality of a request. An example of this would be referring to a law or internal policy to support a request.

This approach may be used to give further credibility to requests made by the network leader to champions. For example: *"Our company policy dictates that we move forward in the manner requested."*

STRATEGY #3 - Coalition

Enlisting other people's support to get a person to take action. For example, a person can convince someone that the action requested is supported by their peers or leaders.

This approach may also be used to give further credibility to requests made by the network leader to champions. For example: *"Our CEO supports this plan of action."*

STRATEGY #4 - Rational Persuasion

Using logical arguments or factual evidence to support the request.

When conducting training, it may be useful to not only educate champions on what their responsibilities are but to explain the justifications that support such responsibilities. This allows champions to better understand their roles and the purpose of the network.

STRATEGY #5 - *Socializing*

Taking a personal interest in others who we are trying to influence. This approach usually entails friendly behavior and attempts to make a personal connection.

While it may be difficult to develop a personal connection with every champion, making attempts to socialize with your champions and build rapport can be helpful in building trust and creating influence.

STRATEGY #6 - *Personal Appeals*

Making a request out of friendship, loyalty, or as a personal favor to the requester. For example: *"We go back a long time, I really need your support here."*

This strategy should generally be *avoided* as a way to influence your champions. Your champions may be serving in their role for a variety of reasons: a sense of obligation to their organization, an interest in the subject area, or a way to show their value and leadership capabilities. Champions should *not* be serving in their role or taking specific action as a personal favor to the network leader. While network leaders may come to develop friendships with their champions, they shouldn't take advantage of such relationships by using personal appeals to motivate their champions.

STRATEGY #7 - *Exchanging*

Giving something of value in return for a request being fulfilled (a quid pro quo). This approach is based on the concept of reciprocity: people tend to return a favor.

In general, a champions network leader should also *avoid* this type of quid pro quo strategy as it sets a bad precedent, making champions believe it's okay to act only if they are given something in return. Regardless of whether the champion is receiving some kind of financial incentive to serve in the role, the relationship between the network leader and champion should almost never be based on reciprocity.

STRATEGY #8 - *Consultation*

Asking the requestee to offer their input as to the action that should be taken. This gives the person a sense of ownership, increasing their motivation to take action.

As a network leader, use this approach to ensure that your champions feel that their opinions are valued and their suggestions are considered. Your champions often understand their business unit, their site, or their department better than you do, so be open to their input. This doesn't mean that as a network leader you must consult with your champions on *everything*, but you should be open to their suggestions and feedback as it relates to their local knowledge or expertise. Champions who feel their input is valued are more likely to stay engaged and take action.

STRATEGY #9 - *Inspirational Appeals*

Focusing on the values or emotions of the person to gain commitment. For example: *"I know how important it is for you to do the right thing, so this is your opportunity to do just that."*

This approach can be used in certain situations, depending on the type of champions network. For example, in a compliance and ethics network, you may appeal to a champion's sense of right versus wrong or their interest in keeping their company or colleagues out of legal trouble. In a cybersecurity network, you may appeal to a champion's desire to keep everyone's information protected. There are also larger values and emotions to leverage in a health and wellness network or an environmental sustainability network.

Champions learn and grow at different rates and develop unique strengths throughout the training process. Be patient and remember that the initial training program is just the beginning. Training and development is an ongoing process that continues throughout the champion's tenure with the network.

After you have completed the initial training program, you're ready for the next step: implementing your champions network.

"Vision without execution is hallucination."

THOMAS EDISON, AMERICAN INVENTOR

7

IMPLEMENTING THE NETWORK

You have leadership support, your structure is in place, and your champions are recruited and trained. It's time to put your champions network into action!

PROMOTING THE NETWORK

Your organization and its employees need to know about the launch of your champions network. A promotional campaign is a great way to introduce your organization to the network and its champions. Many creative ways exist to make sure your champions become known and easily recognized across your organization. Below are a few ideas on how to promote your champions network.

Develop a Brand Identity

A logo for your champions network will increase recognition across the organization. Use this logo to develop a brand identity in email signature lines, intranet postings, newsletters, posters, internal social media, and other communication platforms. Here is an example of a real champions network logo, from Digital Kent, in England:

Send a Formal Announcement

The launch of your champions network is best accompanied by a formal organizational announcement. Your company's internal communications team should be consulted about the best channels by which to make this announcement and how they can assist in your efforts.

In the announcement, provide a brief explanation of the network, its purpose, and the role of champions. Depending on the size of the network, you may want to include the names of all champions in this communication. Also, it may make sense to follow up with targeted announcements letting employees know the champions assigned to their region or department. This type of announcement could also include the following:

- Contact information (phone numbers, email addresses) for champions.
- A link to an internal website dedicated to the champions network.
- Individual or group pictures of champions along with short bios.
- A message to managers and department heads encouraging them to announce the network and its champions during team meetings.
- Information on how interested employees can become future champions.

Other Promotional Ideas

- "Spotlight articles" on individual champions in internal company publications and postings.
- Signage to put in champions' work areas that identify them as champions.
- Lanyards for champions' ID badges that identify them as champions.
- Any number of products that champions can use or wear to publicize their role (e.g., collared shirts, coffee mugs, notebooks).

CONTINUED COMMUNICATION WITH CHAMPIONS

A critical element in your network's successful implementation and operation is to remain in frequent communication with your champions. Your champions network will mature more quickly and be more effective if you, as the network leader, facilitate continued communication and knowledge sharing. Continued communication can include several different channels (as discussed later in this chapter); however, the *simplest* method is to schedule recurring meetings with your champions throughout the year. These meetings can be used for any of the following purposes:

- Addressing emerging issues, questions, or concerns that arise in the network.
- Communicating new and relevant content to champions.
- Providing lessons learned and outcomes achieved from specific cases.
- Giving champions the tools they need to be more successful in their role—training, stories, guides, best practices, templates, etc.
- Gathering feedback from your champions.
- Making champions feel that they have your continued support.

- Providing positive reinforcement to champions that affirms the impact of their efforts.

Your champions network will mature more quickly and be more effective if you, as the network leader, facilitate continued communication and knowledge sharing.

Communication between network leaders and champions is a two-way street, with leaders eager to listen to their champions about what is working well and what isn't. What's keeping them from being successful? Where are the pain points? Where is the resistance or concern? As a network leader, you are responsible for recording these and responding accordingly. The willingness to take constructive input from your champions makes your network stronger and more efficient over time.

Communication Channels

Champions should be given the flexibility to use different channels to communicate with their network leader, their fellow champions, and their colleagues, including:

Company Intranet Sites

A champions network page open to all employees provides an overview of the program, its champions, their locations, and their contact information. Also consider a private group page for champions, including channels to communicate and a resource library with handbooks, guides, templates, and meeting recordings.

Video Conferencing

In-person interaction isn't always feasible or preferable, so virtual-communications options (e.g., Teams or Zoom) should remain an alternative way to interact and train. Schedule a monthly or quarterly forum so champions have an opportunity to share feedback and ask questions in real time. In virtual conferencing scenarios, several factors to consider include group size, the purpose of meetings, the frequency of sessions, time zones, language barriers, interactivity of the participants (e.g., cameras on or off), chat functions, the use of breakout rooms and polls, and ways to involve those champions or employees who cannot access a computer.

Collaborative Tools

Different virtual collaborative tools are available that allow network leaders to connect with their champions or allow champions to communicate and share information with their colleagues in real time. Tools such as Mentimeter and Survey Monkey are just a few of the platforms that can be used to create interactive experiences where champions can gather necessary information and create reports they can share with their network leader and fellow champions.

Social Media

Champions are encouraged to engage with their fellow champions and colleagues via internal social media sites. Engagement on such sites can be monitored/measured by the network leader (number of postings, views, likes, etc.).

E-Newsletter

Distribution of a quarterly e-newsletter is an effective way to communicate with champions. The newsletter can include a summary of recent achievements, links to resources, new action items, upcoming milestones, and network developments.

Communication Tips for Network Leaders

- ✓ Monitor milestones and important achievements of the network.
- ✓ Start each meeting with a brief story, guideline, or tip.

✓ Pick a monthly subtheme within the overall topic of the network (e.g., in an anti-corruption champions network, the monthly subtheme could be gifts and entertainment; in a data-protection champions network, the monthly subtheme could be the use of central file sharing or personal devices).

✓ Send a regular email asking champions for feedback and if they have any questions or concerns.

✓ Use personal stories to help illustrate points.

✓ Set up individual calls with champions that allow for open and transparent conversations.

✓ Set up network group calls (sometimes *without* the network leader present) to allow champions to share and learn from each other.

✓ Use a consistent reporting format or template (this can be shared with champions via a central file-sharing platform) that all champions can use when they need to escalate a potential violation or a sensitive topic.

✓ Ask champions to complete short self-assessments or surveys from time to time in order to gather information on their experiences and where there is room for improvement in the operation of the network.

✓ Keep track of champions' participation in meetings and other network events.

✓ Provide consistent language to champions so they can, in turn, maintain consistency in the messaging they provide to their local colleagues.

✓ Provide champions with presentation decks or individual slides they can use when disseminating information at the local or department level.

✓ Compile and provide a list of frequently asked questions (FAQs) to champions so they have answers to common questions and can be prepared to answer them; update these FAQs as needed.

✓ Give champions coaching and guidance to be better communicators—consider bringing in outside experts or consultants annually to supplement this communications training.

✓ Make yourself available to hear your champions' questions and concerns. Pay attention and *really* listen.

✓ Be clear in the information you provide. When necessary, err on the side of over-explaining—while more information doesn't necessarily entail better information, it may help to prevent misinformation from circulating.

✓ Be prepared to answer difficult questions. If you don't have the right information or don't know the answer, pledge to provide it as soon as you can. Don't let your champions' questions go unanswered.

✓ Counter rumors with fact-based information.

✓ Maintain an organizational chart or list (that can be easily updated) of all champions, preferably arranged by region, site, and department. Make this chart available to all champions and everyone in your organization.

✓ Ensure that your meetings are organized and efficient by putting together a meeting agenda. Here's an agenda template to use for a one-hour meeting with your champions:

TOPIC AND TIME	AGENDA ITEM
Opening: 5 minutes	Provide quick tip and review agenda
Updates: 10 minutes	Discuss project statuses and open items
Activity: 15 minutes	Conduct team-building activity or training
Actions: 15 minutes	Discuss new information and action items
Questions: 10 minutes	Answer questions and address concerns
Closing: 5 minutes	Tell a story and thank the champions

EVALUATING AND ADJUSTING THE NETWORK

Champions networks are not static. They should be designed to adjust to changing conditions and feedback received from leaders, colleagues, and the champions themselves. As the network leader, be open to ways to improve your network to keep it effective and relevant to the organization.

It's important to review many elements of your champions network annually, if not more often, including:

- ✓ The selection criteria for champions.
- ✓ The roles and responsibilities of champions.
- ✓ The performance of individual champions.
- ✓ The effectiveness of your training program.
- ✓ The available methods for communicating and reporting.

> Champions networks are not static. They should be designed to adjust to changing conditions and feedback received from leaders, colleagues, and the champions themselves.

Below are some additional considerations to keep in mind as you evaluate and adjust your network accordingly.

Changing Out Champions

After a specified period of time (usually every year or two), new champions should be welcomed into the organization to replace existing champions. This process will never operate *exactly* as planned—some champions may decide to leave the network before their tenure officially ends, while others may be asked to leave their role early.

Adding new champions allows fresh eyes to come into your network and means your ideas and initiatives will continue to spread even further. Your new champions likely have new network connections, as do those connections, and so on down the line. Don't be too sad to see your existing champions leave, as you may find that former champions continue to serve as informal advocates for your program, initiatives, and ideas.

Benchmarking

In addition to taking feedback directly from your champions, one of the most effective ways to continually evaluate your network is to benchmark with other existing champions networks in your organization or externally. Benchmarking with other network leaders on how they developed, implemented, and operate their champions networks can provide valuable insight into the development and success of your own network. Be sure to piggyback off their good ideas and, with their permission, use resources and templates they have developed. Knowledge sharing is a crucial part of any champions network, so a logical step in the improvement of your own network is to be open to sharing your knowledge and lessons learned (the good and the bad) with other networks.

Keeping Your Champions Engaged

Even a champions network that is well supported, structured, and managed is likely to encounter some challenges along the way. One of the most common challenges to address is: How do you keep your champions engaged?

Provide Access to Professional Development Opportunities

There's a good chance your champions are motivated to serve based on the opportunity to develop their skill set or advance their reputation or visibility within the organization. Depending on these motivations (and your budget), look for opportunities to continually engage such champions in professional networking and development opportunities. For example, bring in an outside consultant to speak to your champions on career development or plan a networking event with senior leaders or C-suite executives, offering champions an opportunity for further visibility within the organization.

Ensure That Your Champions See Their Input in Action

While you should be listening to constructive feedback from all your champions, it serves you well as the network leader to find ways of taking affirmative steps to respond to such feedback. Even if it's on a small scale at first, champions appreciate this. In other words, don't just be a sounding board, take action.

Give Your Champions "Homework"

Since nobody likes homework, maybe don't call it that. However, you can be proactive as the network leader in giving your champions *specific* tasks. This helps to avoid complacency among your champions. For example, instead of simply asking your champions to *"continue engaging with employees and spreading awareness,"* you can assign them to:

- Work on a specific project of importance.
- Investigate a new issue that has arisen.
- Conduct research on a specific topic.
- Have a conversation with a department leader.

Make Sure Champions See the Impact of Their Work

If a champion was involved in spotting a violation or escalating a specific concern, keep them up to date and informed as to its status. After an issue is escalated and no longer within the champion's control, the champion may still have an interest in knowing if and how it was resolved. Champions should be made to feel part of the process from beginning to end.

Incentives and Rewards

Incentives drive behavior, so recognize and reward champions for their work throughout the year. Whether or not you have formal incentives built into the champions role, there are all sorts of ways to show appreciation and recognition that will help keep your champions engaged and active participants in the network. Human Resources may be able to advise on what rewards and incentives resonate most with champions, or you can gather your own data in a survey. You might be surprised at what motivates people to become involved and active champions. Incentives, rewards, and recognitions can be as diverse as the champions in your network, so ensure that you have a variety of options to keep your champions motivated. While you have an entire team of champions to account for, try to recognize every champion as an individual and find ways to incentivize or reward the efforts that each has made toward the network's overall success.

Here are some ways to show recognition to your champions (some of these may require coordination with Human Resources and the champion's manager):

- Tie the champion's role to a salary increase or annual bonus for the year.
- Issue a spot bonus or other form of cash payment for a specific job well done.
- Create a monthly or annual *Champions Network Award* for the most valuable champion in each region or department, or for the overall "MVC" (Most Valuable Champion) of the network.
- Recognize champions in articles and postings featured on company intranet sites, office screens, posters, or emails.
- Provide verbal recognition at a company-wide meeting, especially a meeting attended by senior-level leaders or executives.
- Send a gift to a champion recognizing an individual project completed or goal accomplished (look through your company's online store to find a variety of such gifts, big and small).
- Pay for a well-performing champion to attend an out-of-town conference related to the subject matter of the network.
- Organize an off-site activity for champions (a sporting event, a movie night, or a dinner) to acknowledge their hard work.
- Ask a senior leader or C-suite executive to send a personalized letter to a champion, thanking them for their commitment to the role.
- Hold an end-of-year celebration with your champions.
- Issue a certificate of achievement.
- Take a champion out to lunch.
- Provide a champion with a formal review that contains substantive and valuable feedback.
- Say *"thank you"* to a champion.

The champions network you implement at the start may look different after only a short time. Be open-minded to input and suggestions that you receive from your champions, as well as any leaders and employees within the organization who interact with your network and your champions. As your network grows, you should expect to receive more feedback. Whether it's positive, negative, or neutral, more feedback means more people within your organization know about your network.

After your champions network is implemented and operational for a period of time, you are ready to begin the final step of the blueprint: measuring your network's success.

"You can only improve what you measure."

TOM PETERS, BUSINESS MANAGEMENT WRITER

8

MEASURING NETWORK SUCCESS

Measuring the success of your program isn't just an exercise in ego. It's an opportunity to demonstrate why your network should continue to receive leadership support and a budget, and how your network can grow and develop in the long term. As with every other aspect of the blueprint, how you measure success will vary from one organization to the next. However, *all* champions networks (regardless of industry, size, or substance) need to measure their success.

> Metrics allow you to keep a finger on the pulse of your champions network and report tangible results to your leadership.

WHY MEASURE?

Developing metrics is a way to track your network's effectiveness, help guide decisions about its continued operation, and provide justification for its continued support and financial investment. Metrics allow you to keep a finger on the pulse of your champions network and report tangible results to your leadership. Most importantly, if you intend to make your champions network a long-term, sustainable initiative that can continue to grow within your organization, gathering metrics is a critical step. Your network can only grow if its impact and added value is clearly understood and appreciated.

TYPES OF MEASUREMENT

The types of metrics available to measure the success of your champions network can be grouped into two categories: quantitative and qualitative.

Quantitative Metrics

Operating Metrics

Operating metrics provide evidence the network is operating as planned. Operating metrics include numbers that relate to:

- Champions appointed, by department and geographical areas.
- Training conducted and percentage of attendance achieved.
- Questions answered or issues handled by champions.
- Projects completed with the support of champions.
- Average length of time champions serve.

Engagement Metrics

Engagement metrics provide evidence showing how employees are engaging with the network. Engagement metrics include:

- Percentage of communications about the network that were opened.
- Number of times the champions network intranet page was viewed.
- Time employees spent on the champions network intranet page.
- Repeat visitors to the champions network intranet page.

- Survey results from employees that can be quantified.
- Number of employee comments on internal posts and message boards.
- Results of quizzes after training has been completed.

Value Metrics

Value metrics provide evidence that the network is a value-add to the organization. Value metrics establish a causal connection between the network and the following:

- Rates of incidents, violations, and reports.
- Operational process improvements.
- Organizational efficiencies or profits.

Behavioral Metrics

Behavioral metrics provide evidence of how the network is changing behaviors or culture. Behavioral metrics include the following:

- Number of reports made to champions.
- Timely closure of corrective actions.
- Time elapsed between an event occurring and a champion becoming aware.

Qualitative Metrics

Qualitative metrics tend to be more substantive in nature, but not as easy to measure in terms of hard numbers or percentages. Qualitative metrics include:

- Feedback from champions.
- Periodic short surveys from champions or employees.
- Stories of success (and failure) collected from champions.

LINKING METRICS TO GOALS

Regardless of which type of metrics you choose to measure success, they should ideally correlate to the overall goals of the network. These goals may include:

Your personal objectives

- ✓ Spreading greater awareness of your ideas.
- ✓ Changing company culture.
- ✓ Creating employee engagement.

Your leadership's objectives

- ✓ Measurable financial impacts.
- ✓ A more knowledgeable employee base.
- ✓ An increase in workforce morale.

The objectives set by the applicable industry standards

- ✓ A decrease in legal violations.
- ✓ An improvement in safety and health concerns.
- ✓ A measurable impact on diversity hiring.

Be sure to share the metrics you collect with your leadership *and* with your champions—let them see their success. After metrics are collected and shared, don't become complacent: use the metrics as a baseline to create new objectives for the coming year. Establish new calls to action, develop higher standards to meet, and raise the bar when it comes to communication and knowledge sharing. Raising expectations allows your champions network to continually grow in size, impact, and influence.

PART III

THE EXAMPLES

"If you think compliance is expensive, try non-compliance."

PAUL McNULTY, FORMER U.S. DEPUTY ATTORNEY GENERAL

9

COMPLIANCE AND ETHICS

The types of champions networks that can be implemented across organizations and communities are virtually unlimited. The final chapters of this book focus on four types of champions networks (each of which, on their own, could include numerous subsets of networks within them). The first type of champions network discussed is one of the most common: Compliance and Ethics (C&E). While this field is relatively broad, let's begin with a couple of basic definitions to set the foundation:

Compliance

The act of obeying a law or rule, especially one that controls a particular industry or type of work.

Ethics

Principles of conduct governing an individual or a group.

How do these broad definitions play out in the context of C&E champions networks? This chapter lays out the case for building a C&E champions network, shows how they operate, explains some of their distinctive characteristics, and offers a few real-world examples of such networks.

WHY BUILD A C&E CHAMPIONS NETWORK?

C&E networks help ensure that an organization is compliant with government-imposed regulations and industry standards, as well as an organization's compliance and ethics policies. A company's ethical standards may go beyond what is required by law, with a C&E network put in place to ensure that the organization's culture comports with this higher standard. Highlighted in this chapter are a few examples of real-world C&E champions networks that have been implemented to meet such regulatory requirements and ethical standards.

One of the reasons why champions networks are a good fit for compliance and ethics is because the field, in general, is not revenue generating (although avoiding fines and reputational damage that come with compliance and ethics violations can certainly *save* your organization a lot of money). Because this function is not revenue generating, there's a greater motivation for organizations to keep C&E overhead low. This often translates into understaffing of C&E roles and underfunding of C&E programs and initiatives.

> Having a greater compliance and ethics presence throughout your organization contributes to a stronger overall compliance culture, local employee engagement, and greater adherence to compliance policies.

Whether or not this tendency of organizations to cut costs when it comes to C&E is well-advised (most C&E professionals would argue that it isn't), this view of the compliance and ethics function can work to your advantage. If you are a C&E professional looking to develop a champions network in your organization, consider this: instead of asking your management or leadership to pay the costs of adding full-time C&E head count, make the argument that a C&E champions network allows the organization to *save* money by leveraging the current employee base to provide needed C&E support. Still, expect some pushback and questions (as you would with any other champions network) and be prepared to respond accordingly.

Because most companies do not have the budget or resources to hire full-time compliance professionals in every region or every site around the world, nor to embed C&E professionals within every department, a C&E champions network serves as a useful resource for filling organizational compliance gaps as well as creating greater compliance awareness. Having a greater compliance and ethics presence throughout your organization contributes to a stronger overall compliance culture, local employee engagement, and greater adherence to compliance policies. Further, champions can be used strategically by a centralized C&E department to spread information and ideas, as well as spot and report local C&E issues and violations.

**National Grid Ethics Liaisons
and Con Edison Ethics Advisors**

Excerpt from:
"Engaging Ethical Ambassadors on the Front Lines"
Notre Dame Deloitte Center for Ethical Leadership

We all know that tone at the top is important: without legitimate, committed support from senior management, even the best ethics program will fail.

But if you're a huge company with multiple locations and operations, how do you spread the message of your values to your most remote employees? How do you tailor the messaging to be relevant to different units with different purposes? And how do you stay aware of what's happening on the ground in each location?

National Grid and Consolidated Edison, Inc., two of the world's largest investor-owned energy companies, have implemented a strategy that might be part of the solution: ethics ambassadors programs. Both companies face the challenge of communicating across multiple geographically-diverse sites, all of which have varied operations and different internal cultures. Through their respective ethics ambassadors programs, these organizations are seeing significant success in engaging their employees in a cohesive mission.

National Grid began the Ethics Liaison Network in 2009 after launching their refreshed code of conduct, *Always Do the Right Thing*. Bill Holzhauer, National Grid's US Director of Ethics and Compliance, says that this launch presented an opportunity to do something new. He explains, "We wanted to create a culture where people were comfortable raising concerns—a culture of trust. We knew that to do this, we would have to build an environment where the employees understood the why of our ethical standards." With this goal in mind, National Grid piloted their Ethics Liaison program.

The role of National Grid Liaisons is to act as resources to their peers, facilitate reporting, and shape corporate ethics and compliance messaging to engage their individual teams. Liaisons receive and disseminate various communications from the Ethics and Compliance Office including a quarterly ethics newsletter, an annual report on their progress, and monthly memos to managers. They conduct programming that includes putting an Ethics Spotlight on employees for exhibiting exceptional ethical behavior and reviewing case studies of scrubbed in-house ethical breaches. Finally, the Liaisons participate in monthly calls to share their progress, challenges, and strategies. They do not fulfill the reporting and investigative functions of the Ethics and Compliance team, but are instead resources to their coworkers and bridges between corporate offices and their units—an ear to the ground for the Ethics and Compliance office. Since its inception, the Ethics Liaison program has multiplied tenfold, becoming an integral part of the ethics program of National Grid.

Like National Grid, Con Edison's ethics ambassadors program evolved from its challenges: the company's diversity of geographic locations and site cultures was limiting their ability to propagate their ethics and compliance messages to their employees. After making the choice to separate their ethics and compliance functions in 2012, they piloted the Values in Action program with 15 advisors. Nadine Rivellese, Con Edison's Director of Business Ethics and Compliance, notes that "the desirable characteristics of an Advisor include good influence among peers, strong interpersonal skills, demonstration of integrity, and a good knowledge of the formal and informal organizational communication channels." The Con Edison approach is similar to National Grid's: the Advisors act as a focus group for the ethical issues in the company, commune regularly to share insights and strategies, and serve as positive resources for employees on integrity-related topics. Like the Ethics Liaisons, the VIA Advisors are responsible for programming and support, but they do not supplant the Business Ethics and Compliance function.

Both National Grid and Con Edison have seen positive effects from their programs. The Directors report that they are better apprised of the ethical climate of their respective organizations, and both programs have been lauded internally. In 2014, National Grid's Ethics Liaisons were recognized by the company's organization-wide Chairman's Award for Excellence, and the President and Chief Operating Officer of Con Edison stated in a recent brief to employees, "Our goal as an organization is to foster a self-correcting culture where issues are raised and addressed at the department level by simply talking to each other. The VIA Advisor network is a resource to help us get there."

So, how can you do this at your organization? First, assess your structure to decide how many ambassadors you need. Should you institute a ratio of 1 ambassador to every 200 employees? Or are your locations so dispersed that you need an ambassador at every location? Next, have leadership nominate ambassadors based on demonstrated integrity in their performance and their relationships, leadership ability, and communication skills. Finally, ensure that managers are prepared to support their ambassadors. Both Rivellese and Holzhauer stress that in a successful program, managers understand the ambassador role, give ambassadors time to fulfill their larger set of duties, and consider their employees' additional efforts when evaluating their performance.

TYPES OF C&E CHAMPIONS NETWORKS

Below are a few different types of compliance champions networks:

- Business compliance.
- Healthcare compliance.
- Anti-corruption compliance.
- Employment compliance.
- Cybersecurity compliance.
- Privacy compliance.

- Safety compliance.
- Environmental compliance.
- Trade compliance.

Many such compliance networks have an element of ethics built into them. In some cases, organizations maintain standalone ethics champions networks.

An example of an ethics champions network can be found at MHP, the largest producer and exporter of chicken in Ukraine. The company specializes in the production of chicken and the cultivation of cereals, as well as other agricultural activities. The MHP Compliance Ambassadors Program is a good example of C&E champions networks that exist in a variety of industries and locations around the world.

MHP Compliance Ambassadors

Excerpt from:
"People Power Extending the Reach
of Corporate Compliance & Ethics"
MHP

How can an organization support large numbers of employees in multiple locations in doing the right thing when faced with an ethical dilemma? This goal remains the key challenge for any responsible and accountable business.

When seeking to manage an effective compliance program for a global and diverse organization like MHP, proper implementation requires support across various locations, countries, or regions where the company does business.

MHP encourages its about 32,000 employees to contribute to integrity in their daily business lives and as members of society. The MHP Compliance Office holds a vital role in ensuring that ethics is part of all business operations and that the core values are embedded and reflected in the organization's culture.

One element of our commitment to growing integrity standards inside and around the company is the MHP Compliance Ambassadors Program.

Whether you call it "Ambassadors Program," "Champions Program," or "Liaison Program," it does the same critically vital thing—spread awareness and broaden the reach of corporate compliance and ethics program by using extra arms, legs, and ears, building an effective C&E network, keeping employees engaged, and most importantly, [ensuring] local "buy-in" from all locations, sharing ideas, and addressing issues that are of particular interest.

The Program helps to:

- Successfully navigate the changing landscape.
- Optimize the organizational structure to maximize effectiveness.
- Attract and retain talents with the highest standards of integrity and work ethics.
- Inspire, sustain, and expand the network of committed and engaged employees in the medium and long term, building in continuous improvement.
- Effectively communicate with the broader workforce.
- [Measure] and assess the Company's Compliance Program and its results.

MHP Compliance Ambassadors are MHP employees assisting senior management in promoting an ethical culture based on shared core values within the organization. Although they liaise with full-time ethics practitioners, they are not part of the Compliance Office[.] Their backgrounds can be diverse, but their responsibilities as Compliance Ambassadors tend to be similar to facilitate conversations on ethics and identify ways in which various parts of the business can work together, providing real impact.

To meet our long-term commitment of sharing best practices investing [in] the sustainable growth of the markets around MHP, we are working on the MHP Compliance Ambassadors Program Best Practices Paper, a guidebook on how Ambassadors Programs work, to support efforts to plan and implement the Compliance Ambassadors (CA) Program or enhance an existing CA program while engaging with customers, suppliers, and other partners. The factors that could make it a successful addition to the organization's arsenal of ethics change interventions are also proposed. In addition, the handbook outlines the responsibilities of ambassadors, defines the key skills they require, describes the training, competencies and theoretical knowledge needed

in the ambassador role, and outlines how such a program can be insti-
tuted within the broader ethics management plan. We also provide some
guidance on how to measure the success of the Program.

WAYS TO UTILIZE YOUR C&E CHAMPIONS

Spread Compliance Awareness

Use your C&E champions to disseminate information and materials, ensuring that important compliance announcements, policies,
and other communications are understood and implemented locally.
Champions can be asked to incorporate C&E talking points into
local staff and departmental meetings, making themselves available to
answer questions or point their colleagues in the direction of helpful
C&E resources and subject-matter experts.

Take Employee Reports

C&E champions are approachable to their colleagues who may have
compliance-related questions or concerns and available to listen to
colleagues who wish to report such concerns. Champions should
be trained by C&E leaders in best practices for taking such reports,
including how to properly escalate matters that may be confidential or
involve a potential violation of law or company policy.

Provide Training

C&E champions are instructed on how to deliver various types of
compliance training and may then be tasked with leading local training
within their departments or sites. This train-the-trainer approach is
more adaptable to some areas of compliance than others, but it should
be considered where a centralized C&E function's resources or time
are at a premium.

Gain Local Insights

While a centralized compliance and ethics function educates C&E champions and uses them to spread awareness at a local level, champions are also encouraged to educate and update the central C&E function on issues that are arising locally in their region, site, or department. C&E champions can serve as the eyes and ears of compliance and ethics at the local level. Champions may be asked to assist compliance leaders in tailoring their messaging ahead of time to certain parts of the business or to explain afterward why certain C&E communications may have failed to resonate at the local level. A champions network is an opportunity for C&E leaders to learn about structural changes to departments, the development of new products, new hiring practices, new ways of working, etc., all of which could have a significant compliance and ethics impact on the organization at large.

Tasks and Functions for C&E Champions

- Participating in risk assessments.
- Providing compliance training.
- Disseminating communications and messaging within their site or functional group.
- Cascading policies and procedures.
- Participating in internal investigations, as deemed appropriate by the Legal Department.
- Leading Compliance & Ethics Week(s).
- Learning to identify (and possibly mitigate) compliance issues.
- Identifying gaps in the compliance program.
- Attending training sessions.
- Providing constructive input and feedback on training, policies, or procedures.
- Helping to draft local policies, procedures, or training.
- Following up with colleagues who have not completed their training.
- Collecting metrics to help determine the success of the network.

- Being the eyes and ears of the C&E Department.
- Spotting red flags to report back to the C&E Department.
- Being a trusted compliance resource for colleagues.
- Taking reports from colleagues regarding compliance concerns or violations.
- Helping to identify, report, manage, and assess the root cause of incidents and working to implement corrective actions.
- Listening to their colleagues' perspective on compliance initiatives.
- Responding to C&E questions and concerns.
- Escalating issues to the C&E or Legal Departments.
- Obtaining information more quickly than the C&E function can because of the trust they have already built at the local or department level.

Tasks and Functions that C&E Champions Should Not Perform

- Acting as compliance "spies" within their department or site.
- Leading investigations of serious legal or ethical violations that should be conducted by an attorney or other subject-matter expert.
- Providing legal advice to fellow employees.
- Making determinations as to whether a specific issue or concern rises to the level of a compliance or legal violation (champions can report such issues, but they should not be unilaterally making such determinations).
- Responsibilities that duplicate those of others in their department or site.

Teradata Ethics and Compliance Advocates

Excerpt from:
"Guide for Building and Sustaining an Effective Champion Program"
Business Ethics Leadership Alliance

Teradata, a U.S. software company, defined the roles of its Ethics and Compliance (E&C) Advocates as they relate to various audiences within the organization:

Responsibilities of Advocates to Teradata
- Be familiar with the Teradata Code of Conduct and E&C program.
- Raise the profile and awareness of the E&C program within the company.

Responsibilities of Advocates to Employees
- Be a role model and lead by example.
- Encourage employees to speak up whenever they have questions or concerns.
- Direct employees to appropriate policies and procedures.
- Facilitate roundtable discussions on ethics issues with employees.

Responsibilities of Advocates to the E&C Department
- Act as conduit between the E&C Department and the business to:
  o Contact new employees shortly after their onboarding to ensure they understand Teradata's commitment to ethics and compliance and are acquainted with Teradata's E&C office and resources.
  o Promote E&C communications and initiatives, regularly share the messages within the framework of their business group.
  o Direct employees to the E&C office with questions or concerns.
  o Facilitate completion of Code of Conduct training for new hires.
  o Bridge cultural and language barriers.

- Assist E&C Department in understanding the organizational structure of their line of business, major areas of exposure, and topics of interest to the business.
- Identify opportunities in the business to train employees, make presentations, or otherwise engage in ethics and compliance.
- Provide feedback on effectiveness of training and communications.
- Attend calls with E&C Department to share feedback and align messaging.
- E&C Advocates should not conduct intake evaluations for ethical concerns, act as an advisor for ethical issues, make determinations as to what constitutes a reportable ethical issue, or conduct investigations. These remain the responsibility of the E&C Department.

THE U.S. DEPARTMENT OF JUSTICE ON CHAMPIONS NETWORKS

In March 2023, the U.S. Department of Justice (DOJ) updated its *Evaluation of Corporate Compliance Programs*. This document serves as guidance for all U.S. organizations to measure their compliance programs against. The 2023 amendments include a paragraph listing the factors that the DOJ considers in determining whether to prosecute companies for compliance violations. This language states, in part:

> *"Prosecutors should examine whether a company has made working on compliance a means of career advancement,* **offered opportunities for managers and employees to serve as a compliance 'champion,'** *or made compliance a significant metric for management bonuses."*

The language makes clear that champions networks are now a DOJ-recommended course of action that companies can take to build a compliant culture *and* mitigate against potential prosecution. The timing could not be better for U.S. organizations to build new C&E champions networks and improve their existing networks.

ESTABLISHING METRICS FOR C&E NETWORKS

In Chapter 8 we discussed how the success of a champions network can be measured. Depending on the current maturity of your compliance program, you may already have compliance metrics from which you can draw. For example, if your organization's C&E Department has been conducting compliance training or sending out compliance surveys to your workforce,

Compliance and ethics "success" can sometimes be hard to measure—that won't stop your leadership from asking to see evidence of it.

you may already be able to gather some compliance-related metrics (quantitative or qualitative) to set a baseline standard that can be measured against.

Compliance and ethics "success" can sometimes be hard to measure—that won't stop your leadership from asking to see evidence of it. Be prepared to find creative but realistic ways of measuring such success, including the following:

An Increase in Requests, Questions, and Comments

A well-implemented C&E champions network increases compliance awareness throughout your company, as measured by a corresponding increase in the number of requests, questions, and comments received via the established communication and reporting channels. You can track and compare this increased communication from the time the champions network is first implemented and throughout its continued growth (every month, every quarter, every year, etc.) to develop quantitative metrics that provide evidence of an increase in compliance awareness. Be sure to account for compliance questions and inquiries that have been successfully closed out.

Survey Results

Internal compliance surveys can contain questions about employees' awareness and understanding of compliance topics as they relate to their job function, department, or the company. Such surveys can also include basic questions asking where employees can find more information and who they can contact with C&E concerns. An employee survey on compliance and ethics that is distributed *before* the implementation of a champions network would, ideally, produce very different and measurable responses than the same survey sent *after* the successful implementation and continued operation of the network. For example, try creating an internal compliance survey with the following types of questions, as provided by the Business Ethics Leadership Alliance:

On a scale of 1 to 5, with 1 indicating *completely unaware* and 5 indicating *extremely aware*, rate the following:

- Your awareness of the specific elements of the policies and procedures related to [C&E topic].
- Your awareness of how to access the policies and procedures related to [C&E topic].
- Your awareness of how to raise questions, concerns, or suggestions concerning [C&E topic].

On a scale of 1 to 5, with 1 indicating *no customization* and 5 indicating *thorough customization*, rate the following:

- How well the [C&E topic] program materials or training have been customized for your function or location.

Alexion Compliance Champions

Excerpt from:
"Compliance Champions"
3BL Media

Every person at Alexion [a pharmaceutical company and subsidiary of AstraZeneca] is accountable for doing the right thing for patients, every day. The Alexion Compliance team is not just tasked with ensuring that we meet this responsibility; they also provide the right guidance, clarity, and resources to help us make decisions with integrity. "Our goal is to make compliance a dynamic aspect of every employee's work and we want to ensure that colleagues can easily connect to and obtain guidance regarding how to interact with internal and external stakeholders and how to make informed, ethical decisions for our business," said Petra Lehmann, Compliance & Ethics, Europe North, UK & Ireland.

To ensure employees across all functions and geographies understand our compliance standards, Alexion has launched a *Compliance Champions* program. Colleagues from a wide range of functions and geographies serve as Compliance Champions, acting as the voice of compliance, sharing best practices, and helping lead compliance-related initiatives. At the same time, they serve as conduits to the global compliance team, listening to local issues and concerns, encouraging a speak-up culture, identifying opportunities to share successes or lessons, and raising needs for new guidance to address situation-specific needs.

Tolga Tanguler, Head of U.S. Commercial, said, "Our compliance standards are hugely valuable to working effectively as a team. They provide us the clarity and clear direction to interpret the right approach for patients. Implementing a network of Compliance Champions brings this process into our local cultures, facilitating a dialogue and guiding the application of compliance concepts to help every employee understand and integrate these principles into their work."

USING INCENTIVES IN C&E NETWORKS

For some business leaders, the idea of using incentives to encourage compliant and ethical behavior can be perceived negatively: *"Why should we pay people extra to comply with the law or to act ethically?".* However, as discussed previously, incentives can also be incredibly influential in recruiting and retaining champions. Rewards and recognition are powerful motivators in creating a compliant and ethical culture in your organization and in your C&E champions network.

Remember, incentives do not necessarily have to be monetary. Stressing the value of helping to protect their company and themselves, as well as the value in being seen as a trusted leader within their region, site, department, or team may be enough of an incentive for some champions.

> *"While incentives are common in business, homes, schools, and other contexts, the use of incentives in the context of compliance and ethics programs has been slow to catch on. This has been true because many compliance and ethics officers don't understand that 'appropriate incentives' are a required element of an effective compliance and ethics program . . . and because too many in management and on boards believe that most employees will naturally 'do the right thing.' Unfortunately, the evidence suggests just the opposite. Without adequate controls and incentives, most of us will (at least occasionally) do the wrong thing."*
>
> **Daniel R. Roach,** Chief Compliance Officer at Optum Insight

The Objections (and Responses) to Incentivizing C&E Champions

Let's review a couple of common objections to incentivizing C&E champions and how you can respond to such objections as the network leader.

Objection 1: Employees Shouldn't Be Rewarded for Doing Their Jobs.

C&E champions are asked to go *beyond* their day-to-day job duties. Champions are given the added responsibility of spreading C&E messaging, initiatives, and ideas across the organization, as well as staying alert to potential C&E violations and helping to escalate them accordingly. Incentives are a recognition of this added responsibility. Incentives can also serve as motivation for champions to continue exhibiting these positive behaviors.

Objection 2: Evaluating the Ethical Behavior of Others Is Too Subjective.

A C&E champion is tasked with evaluating how employees have held up to the ethical standards of their organization. In this respect, the ethical behavior of employees is only as subjective as the standards that the organization sets for its employees. There's no reason why a well-trained C&E champion can't use such standards as a litmus test to observe and evaluate fellow employees' behavior.

Even if ethics can be somewhat subjective, there are plenty of C&E objectives and goals that can be measured, both quantitatively and qualitatively:

- Has a compliant and ethical environment been promoted?
- Has compliance and ethics messaging been successfully communicated?
- Are employees more aware of compliance and ethics policies and procedures now that a champions network has been implemented?

Perhaps the most powerful response to either of the two objections above is that the U.S. government *recommends* the use of incentives in corporate C&E programs:

> *"The organization's compliance and ethics program shall be promoted and enforced consistently throughout the organization through . . . appropriate incentives to perform in accordance with the compliance and ethics program."*

2004 revisions to the U.S. Federal Sentencing Guidelines

"The design and implementation of compensation schemes play an important role in fostering a compliance culture. Prosecutors may consider whether a company has incentivized compliance by designing compensation systems that defer or escrow certain compensation tied to conduct consistent with company values and policies."

2023 revisions to the U.S. DOJ Evaluation
of Corporate Compliance Programs

The post-COVID changes in our current work environment provide even more reasons to implement a C&E champions network. C&E champions can play a role (if approved by their network leader) in helping to address many of the problems their colleagues may be facing—for example, fatigue from the blurred lines between work life and personal life, or challenges that employees may face in becoming more socially isolated at home. Consider having your C&E champions utilize their role to form connections with those co-workers who might otherwise feel disconnected in this new normal.

"Nature has given us all the pieces required to achieve exceptional wellness and health, but has left it to us to put these pieces together."

DIANE McLAREN, NATURAL HEALTH PRACTITIONER

10

HEALTH AND WELLNESS

Research has demonstrated that unhealthy lifestyle behaviors contribute to poor health outcomes, increased healthcare costs, loss of productivity, and problems with absenteeism in the workplace. The U.S. Centers for Disease Control and Prevention now promote the workplace as *"an important setting for health protection, health promotion, and disease prevention programs."* As a result, organizations now invest in a variety of workplace health and wellness programs. Many such programs involve the incorporation of health and wellness (H&W) champions networks that work to strengthen and spread a culture of health within an organization. H&W champions are employees who have a passion for promoting health and wellness among their colleagues. They provide grassroots support for corporate H&W programs by promoting the various activities and initiatives within the program, advocating for healthy worksite policies, providing peer encouragement, and leading by example.

H&W champions promote an organization's health and wellness programs at their local worksites, communicating information to colleagues while providing ongoing feedback to leadership. When these employee advocates come together in a champions network, they can be a catalyst in creating a more health-conscious work environment, encouraging their co-workers to improve their overall health and well-being, and helping their organizations better manage healthcare costs.

THE BENEFITS OF H&W INITIATIVES IN THE WORKPLACE

Several research studies have shown the impact coworkers have on promoting and supporting health and wellness in the workplace setting, including:

Escoffier, Kegler, and Alcantara (2011)

Researchers found the importance of support from worksite peers to encourage changes in eating and weight among employees in a small rural worksite in Georgia.

Allen, Stoddard, Mays, and Sorensen (2001)

Peer health advisors were trained to serve as role models (disseminating information, providing social support, and facilitating screening processes) for breast and cervical cancer screening to female colleagues at multiple worksites. Participants in the program had a significantly greater cervical cancer screening rate than did comparison group participants.

Bondi and Bercovitz (2013)

Researchers observed the positive impacts of peer support provided to individuals in a study that focused on the benefits of stopping smoking.

Webb, Shakeshaft, Sanson-Fisher, and Harvard (2009)

Effective results were observed by researchers in a review of worksite interventions addressing alcohol abuse.

ADA Wellness Ambassadors

Excerpt from:
"Wellness Ambassadors to Support Peer Dentists
Who May Be Struggling"
ADA News

The ADA [American Dental Association] is unveiling the first cohort of dental professionals who have been called to serve on its new initiative called the Wellness Ambassador Program, in which volunteers will work to ensure that peer dentists struggling with health obstacles are aware of support services.

Chief among the ambassadors' messaging is that members and non-members can download the ADA Dentist Well Being Program Directory for free through the ADA Store to find their state program director contact information, with all calls or emails kept strictly confidential.

The directory contains the contact information for the well-being programs offered in the 50 states and the District of Columbia.

Kami Dornfeld, D.D.S., chair of the ADA's Dental Wellness Advisory Committee, said that the 2021 Dentist Well-Being Survey Report, commissioned by the ADA Council on Dental Practice, was troubling in that it revealed that the percentage of dentists diagnosed with anxiety more than tripled in 2021 compared with 2003.

"The survey results clearly showed that dentists continue to be burdened with mental and emotional health concerns, and many at risk of burnout," Dr. Dornfeld said. "The ADA wants dentists, their teams and families to readily find counsel and compassion. Mental health is an ongoing process deserving of nurturing, so creating a team of wellness ambassadors is one way the ADA can continue to build a lifeline for those in need."

As part of a year-long onboarding commitment, the first group of ADA Wellness Ambassadors came together for in-person training at the ADA Headquarters in Chicago in November.

Both ADA President George Shepley, D.D.S., and ADA Executive Director Raymond Cohlmia, D.D.S., greeted the wellness ambassadors at the November training, stressing how crucial the ambassadors' role was.

"This is such important work," Dr. Shepley told the gathering. "I'm grateful we're doing this. We have to take care of our family."

"What you're doing is just a start," Dr. Cohlmia added. "We start today. You'll be changing people's lives."

While the wellness ambassadors will not provide the support a clinical professional would offer, the volunteers serve as advocates to facilitate connections with clinical professionals and other resources.

The ambassadors represent different districts and practice modalities, ranging from dentists at federally qualified health centers to large group practices. Ms. Morrison represents the families of dental professionals through the Alliance of the American Dental Association; she is president of the organization.

The volunteers include Dr. Foster, who drafted Resolution 95H-2021, Prioritizing Mental Health of Dentists, passed by the 2021 House of Delegates.

"The ADA and dentistry are like a family to me," said Dr. Foster. "I believe we discover our passions in life from experience. I lost one of my best friends, a member of the dental family, to suicide. I want to do everything in my power to keep our family safe and being a wellness ambassador lets me honor his memory and take action towards my passion of prioritizing mental health for all, especially dentists."

Fellow ambassador Dr. Barrera is a yoga instructor as well as a public health dentist, and said he agreed to be an ambassador to better the life of new and more experienced dentists alike.

"The better we are, the better the care is for our patients," he said.

Dr. Hung had a personal reason for becoming an ambassador. She said her teenage son entered high school just as the COVID-19 pandemic hit.

"It was hard for him to adjust," she said.

Throughout 2023, ambassadors will gain additional awareness of support resources through participating in online webinars presented by a range of professionals as well as group discussion forums.

Ambassadors will impact their communities by providing a minimum of three projects aligned with the purpose of the program. Opportunities include the potential to collaborate with state and local dentists and association leadership to offer presentations, interviews, or contribute articles to their local newsletters.

TYPES OF H&W INITIATIVES IN THE WORKPLACE

Health and Wellness champions networks incorporate their initiatives in different ways throughout an organization. Below are a few examples of creative and impactful types of H&W engagement in the workplace.

Provide information on updates or changes to company wellness benefits, such as:

Company gym memberships, changes to insurance providers, and insurance discounts for employees who participate in workplace health programs.

Take initiatives to provide space for health and wellness at work, such as:

Healthy dining options, creating walking paths and stress-relief areas.

Host internal health and wellness events, such as:

Health fairs, educational seminars, fitness campaigns, and health lunch-and-learns.

Organize fitness activities in the office or the community, such as:

Charity runs, softball games, and lunchtime walking groups.

Support stress management and relief initiatives, such as:

Work-life balance workshops, monthly massages, and weekly yoga sessions.

Coordinate on-site health screenings, such as:

Flu vaccines, blood drives, and blood pressure stations.

FINDING AND TRAINING YOUR H&W CHAMPIONS

Informal health advocates already exist in your employee population—you just have to find them, train them, and make them a part of your champions network. Training your H&W champions may include any or all of the following, as provided by ShapeUp:

A Health and Wellness Champions Handbook

Create a handbook that includes a schedule of H&W promotions and activities for the year, copies of handouts, key points of contact, FAQs, and a comprehensive list of H&W benefits, programs, and services available to employees.

> Informal health advocates already exist in your employee population—you just have to find them, train them, and make them a part of your champions network.

Health and Wellness Objectives

Lay out the goals for your H&W strategy as well as the areas that champions can directly influence and facilitate. Common goals might include extending the reach of your H&W program to all sites, determining individual site needs, and incorporating H&W into each site's culture. If using specific data to measure the success of your network goals throughout the year, explain those metrics to your champions ahead of time.

Health and Wellness Vendors

Give champions an overview of what's available from these vendors and how their offerings fit into the organization's wellness strategy. Point out services that the champions will be promoting.

Health and Wellness Resources

Provide educational materials around peer counseling and behavior change. Focus on real-world applications a champion can use in day-to-day interactions with co-workers. Confidentiality and privacy issues can be addressed in these materials.

State Employee Wellness Program (SEWP) Champions

Excerpt from:
"Starting a Wellness Program at Your Worksite"
Mississippi State Department of Health

During the 2010 Mississippi Legislative Session, Senate Bill 2646 was passed, creating the State Employee Wellness Program (SEWP). The SEWP is intended for all state employees that participate in the State and School Employees' Health Insurance Plan and is administered by the Mississippi State Department of Health's Office of Preventive Health.

The program has a mission to educate on the most costly and prevalent health care claims, including information addressing lifestyle factors, chemical use, physical activity, healthy eating, and disease prevention.

The SEWP encourages state agencies to utilize and promote policy, environmental, and worksite system changes that encourage employees to make healthy choices and adopt healthy behaviors. Some health policy examples to encourage healthy living include the promotion of tobacco-free workplaces; providing adequate breastfeeding facilities for working mothers at the workplace and healthy catering for meetings/events. Some environmental change strategies include the promotion of healthy food options in vending machines, fitness rooms, stairwell promotion, and walking trails/routes.

State Agency Wellness Champions and Councils

The State Employee Wellness Program requires each state entity to designate an employee to serve as the "wellness champion or wellness liaison" between the agency and the State Employee Wellness Program Director.

Wellness Champion Responsibilities

- Coordinate available resources to educate employees about making healthier lifestyle and wellness choices.
- Organize activities to assist employees in learning new skills to reach their personal health goals.
- Attend State Employee Wellness Program learning opportunities, including webinars, trainings, and conferences.
- Work with agency leadership to provide a supportive work environment to assist employees in reducing negative health behaviors.
- Conduct an annual needs assessment to align worksite wellness activities to employee needs.
- Annually report progress toward a comprehensive model worksite wellness program to the State Employee Wellness Program Director.

Wellness Champions are also responsible for the development of a wellness council composed of employees and managers of their respective agency to implement a wellness program based on best practices. Key steps in creating a wellness committee are to:

- Define the wellness committee's composition
- Recruit members
- Establish committee procedures and ground rules
- Gain leadership support

GUIDANCE FROM WEBMD

WebMD, a well-known online publisher of news and information pertaining to health and wellness, offers the following steps and timeline for developing an effective health and wellness champions network (you'll notice that many of the steps track closely with the blueprint provided in this book):

Steps to Develop an H&W Champions Network

Step #1 - Win Management Support

Leadership support for a culture of health is critical. Senior management controls the budget, operations, and communications, so now is the time to get the decision-makers on board.

Step #2 - Find Passionate Volunteers

While some organizations find it beneficial to appoint champions, a bigger impact on the culture can be seen with a network of volunteers who are already invested in their personal well-being.

Step #3 - Handpick Your Team

You may find that some individuals—despite their enthusiasm—may lack the proper skill set to become champions. An application process can go a long way toward finding qualified ambassadors who are willing to put in the extra time and effort to make your well-being program successful.

Step #4 - Identify Promising Recruits

Champions should be comfortable recruiting support, speaking in meetings, and proactively engaging others. They should be organized and willing to make a reasonable time commitment. Champions needn't be in perfect health, but they should feel passionate about the importance of good health. Finally, champions should be positive people who want to promote well-being.

Step #5 - Look for Funding

While you can run a well-being champions network with minimal funding or none at all, it can be challenging. Inform senior management about the funds you need, but also show a willingness to work with what's initially available. Early successes in the network can have a positive influence on future budgets.

Step #6 - Build Your Network Structure

A dedicated network manager is responsible for your company's well-being program and for training the champion leads. Champion leads represent specific divisions, departments, or regions for your organization. They head up a team of local champions on worksite- and company-wide initiatives. This role involves a significant time commitment, including regular monthly meetings with champions.

Champions are the individuals who work to communicate and support well-being activities at local worksites or key locations. All departments should be represented and individuals of different languages and cultures should be included.

Step #7 - Train Your Champions

Host a kickoff training that covers your overall well-being mission and key messages for champions to deliver to their populations. Then follow up with a second, more in-depth session.

Step #8 - Keep Your Team Engaged

Once you've created your champions network, all participants should have the tools they need. Schedule monthly meetings where champion leads work with local champions on the following objectives:

- Gather feedback from the various locations and populations.
- Provide support and documentation for company-wide initiatives.
- Share ideas about improving engagement and implementing challenges.
- Review outcomes to track progress or highlight areas of improvement.
- Send out a quarterly newsletter with updated program information.
- Invite their team to special events, like a seminar or a healthy lunch.
- Create a guide with information on incorporating health and wellness tips.

Step #9 - Track Metrics

Measure the impact of your champions network. Is it providing the desired value to the company? There are many ways to measure success, so consider which metrics make the biggest impression on your organization's leadership.

Timeline to Develop an H&W Champions Network

90 Days to Launch

- ✓ Get management support and finalize funding, if applicable.
- ✓ Announce you are creating a champions network: hang flyers, send emails, have conversations, and encourage people to spread the word.
- ✓ Accept and review applications for champions, if applicable.
- ✓ Collaborate with vendors and finalize supporting materials for the major yearly campaigns (open enrollment, health assessments, well-being fairs).

60 Days to Launch

- ✓ Begin the interview and selection process.
- ✓ Finalize supporting materials for major yearly campaigns.
- ✓ Begin monthly meetings with vendors to maintain support for campaigns.
- ✓ Plan kick-off meeting logistics, including date, time, and venue.
- ✓ Create or order kick-off meeting materials for champions.

30 Days to Launch

- ✓ Finalize and select your champions.
- ✓ Finalize kick-off meeting details.
- ✓ Sign off on final supporting materials for major yearly campaigns.
- ✓ Initiate monthly meetings with well-being vendors.

Launch!

✓ Hold a kick-off meeting with your champions.
✓ Announce your champions to the company, individual sites, or departments.
✓ Start the first initiative: Complete a health assessment.
✓ Be available for questions and support.

Ongoing

✓ Communicate with management to keep their support.
✓ Build your culture of well-being.
✓ Coordinate approved well-being initiatives.
✓ Review metrics.
✓ Maintain monthly meetings with your network and with vendors.

Buckeye Wellness Innovators

Excerpt from:
"Workplace Wellness Champions:
Lessons Learned and Implications for Future Programming"
Building Healthy Academic Communities Journal

The team of wellness champions at The Ohio State University is called the Buckeye Wellness Innovators. The program is implemented out of the Office of the Vice President for Health Promotion and Chief Wellness Officer (CWO) and co-facilitated by the Director of Health Promotion and Wellness Program Manager. The Innovator program began in January of 2012. There are 464 Wellness Innovators across the university, representing 160 academic and medical center departments/units.

Roles and Responsibilities

Buckeye Wellness Innovators are University and medical center faculty and staff who have a special interest in facilitating a culture and environment of wellness in their college, unit, or department. They champion university-wide wellness initiatives in their departments and advance the One University Health and Wellness strategic plan. Innovators are responsible for communicating health and wellness activities to their colleagues, encouraging and motivating faculty and staff to participate in wellness initiatives, engage in healthy lifestyle practices, utilize wellness resources, and plan and conduct wellness activities in their colleges, departments or units. They are required to devote two to three hours per month to the program and to coordinate their efforts with the co-facilitators and human resources personnel when applicable to ensure health and wellness communications are aligned. Innovators who are faculty at the university have the opportunity to count the Innovator role towards their service requirements.

One University Approach to Wellness

The vision of the wellness program at Ohio State is: "To be the healthiest university on the globe." To achieve this ambitious vision, the One University Health and Wellness Council provides strategic leadership and direction for health and wellness initiatives across the university. The council is led by the University's Vice President for Health Promotion and Chief Wellness Officer and is comprised of key leaders across the University who have responsibility for various aspects of health and wellness for faculty, staff and students along with representation from faculty, staff, students, and University communications. The University embraces nine dimensions of wellness and uses this comprehensive model as a guide for designing, implementing, and evaluating wellness programs and services for students, faculty and staff based on the socioecological framework to guide evidence-based intervention and outcomes assessment. Innovators promote wellness programs and resources designed to enhance faculty and staff wellness among all nine dimensions throughout the calendar year. In addition, the socio-ecological framework adopted by the University represents a vital piece of its health promotion efforts, targeting multiple levels of impact: individual, social networks and family, culture and environment, and policy. Oftentimes, when Innovators plan wellness activities for their department, they address one or more of the levels mentioned above.

Recruitment

To recruit new Wellness Innovators, the program facilitators disseminate a call for Innovators three times per year. Recruitment information
is sent out through a series of emails: From the daily internal university
system to all faculty and staff; from the CWO to University deans and
vice presidents (VP); to human resource professionals in colleges and
VP units; and finally, to current Wellness Innovators and individuals who
have participated in University health and wellness programs. Wellness
Innovators are self-nominated or are nominated by a manager/super-
visor or existing Wellness Innovator for this volunteer role. Innovators
must have approval from their supervisor to participate in the program.

Once recruited, new Innovators attend a four-hour orientation.
At this orientation, new Innovators are introduced to the University's
wellness vision, mission and core goals. They also review the wellness
program components applicable to the faculty and staff, educational
health promotion offerings, wellness services and the employee assistance program. They then receive a detailed description of their new
responsibilities. Following the orientation, program facilitators contact
the new Innovators to schedule a one-hour strategy session. The program facilitators outline role expectations and work with the Innovators
to construct a plan for their department or unit over the next 12 months.
The Innovator's manager/supervisor is invited to the meeting to ensure
their direct leader is aware of the responsibilities and expected time
commitment of being an Innovator and is supportive of their role. In
early 2017, the program facilitators implemented a new retention effort,
which includes meeting with each Innovator on an annual basis to discuss successes and challenges to their role.

Demographics of the Innovators

Currently, there are 464 Innovators at The Ohio State University, 224
represent the medical center and 240 represent the academic side of
the university. The majority of Innovators are University staff (447)
and 15 are faculty. Innovators are located at all five regional campuses
of the university and ten work in Ohio's county positions within the
University's extension offices. A majority of Innovators are female (over
85 percent).

Strategy Sessions

Following the orientation, the program facilitators meet with the Innovator or Innovators if there is more than one in a department, for a strategy session. Their discussion includes the following areas:

1. The environment of the department: Manager support, perceptions of stress levels, perceived interest among colleagues in engaging in healthy behaviors, and demographics. The Innovator has the option to conduct a short baseline survey, asking colleagues which areas of wellness are of most interest.
2. Overall adopted university wellness strategies.
3. A description of their main responsibilities (communication, encouragement, and planning activities), and expectations. A checklist of annual activities is given to the innovators during the meeting for tracking their activities and efforts.
4. Examples of what other Innovators are implementing.
5. Funding opportunities for supporting department/unit-specific wellness efforts.
6. Collaborating with human resources where appropriate.
7. Communication resources.
8. Incentives and benefits that are exclusively available to them such as complimentary participation in the Health Athlete corporate program.
9. Action items for follow-up.

The session takes approximately one hour. Program facilitators follow-up with the Innovators throughout the year to provide ongoing support.

Financial Support through Funding Opportunities

Innovators are invited to apply for grants, up to $500, to support the on-going efforts to influence the wellness culture and environment of their department/unit. This biannual funding opportunity encourages Innovators to submit a proposal to fund activities or programs that promote physical activity, healthy eating or emotional well-being among their colleagues. Thus far, 30 Innovators have received grants to support their proposals. The program facilitators require a written report one (1) year from the date of implementation. Innovators are required to track participation, and are highly encouraged to report implementation details and outcomes data.

Strategic Communication

Communication is an important aspect of the Wellness Innovators program; however, efforts need to be strategic. Once a month, the co-facilitator of the program sends out an email with a couple of high priority health and wellness announcements. The second co-facilitator creates a monthly email newsletter that Innovators can share with their departments. In addition, the private Facebook group allows Innovators to share ideas, pictures, activities and resources. The program facilitators also contribute content to the page. Twice a year, a webinar is held to update Innovators on current and upcoming events. Biannual luncheons spotlight Innovators' efforts, provide opportunities for brainstorming ways to overcome challenges, and host motivational guest speakers to re-energize the group.

Unique Opportunities

Innovators have the benefit of attending a free two-day energy management course as a part of their role and are highly encouraged to utilize this benefit. The energy management course, called Health Athlete, mirrors the Human Performance Institute's Corporate Athlete program (2011), and is part of a formal partnership with Johnson & Johnson, owners of the Corporate Athlete program. Not only does the Health Athlete program help develop their personal energy management skills but allows them to take back some strategies for achieving high levels of wellbeing to their departments and colleagues.

Manager and Supervisor Support

In 2016, the health promotion experts at Ohio State began efforts to engage mid-level managers and supervisors in the University's health and wellness initiative. This effort is currently ongoing. Managers and supervisors are essential to the success of the overall program because they provide support and encouragement to those that work for them (i.e., a manager allowing staff to attend a wellness fair on work time, or encouraging staff to take 15 minutes during their work hours to get a biometric screening). We have noted that if the Innovator's manager/ supervisor does not support their employee to engage in worksite wellness activities, the wellness efforts in that department are likely to stall. When the manager/supervisor does not receive the support that is needed to fulfill their role, they tend to become disengaged from the program. Therefore, the facilitators of the program ask all Innovators to obtain approval from their direct supervisor before entering the program. Managers/supervisors also are invited to attend the one-hour strategy session as well as some or all of the orientation so that they are aware of the responsibilities and expected time commitment of the Innovator role and can provide support. In the event that a supervisor does not grant permission for their employee to engage in the Innovator program, the facilitators of the program provide the manager with additional information, such as the University president's wellness goal, to further increase her/his understanding. This is generally received well and permission is granted.

Activities Being Conducted by the Innovators

The program facilitators instruct Innovators to create and implement activities that focus on one or more of the nine dimensions of wellness. Innovators promote several areas of wellness, including: Healthy eating, physical activity and stress management/coping, but are able to promote wellness in other dimensions, such as financial, social, spiritual, environmental, occupational and intellectual. With 464 Innovators enrolled in the program, a wide variety of health and wellness activities are implemented within their departments/units. For example, Innovators often plan healthy food demonstrations and potlucks, lead teams for physical activity competitions, and encourage stairwell usage. Many Innovators enlist health promotion experts, such as members of the Chief Wellness Officer's wellness team or the university's health plan health coaches, to present on wellness topics. These presentations are often done during the lunch hour or in staff and faculty meetings. Innovators plan yoga and other fitness classes in their departments/units, and work with the program facilitators, colleagues, university health and wellness service departments, and at times, local businesses to secure instructors and space. Additionally, Innovators are provided with toolkits, such as the American Heart Association's Healthy Workplace Food and Beverage Toolkit, which enables them to use evidence-based information when selecting healthy food options for work-related meetings and functions.

Assessing Engagement and Impact

To date in the literature, few studies have been conducted to assess the level of engagement necessary and impact of wellness champion teams on health and wellness outcomes. In order to further the field and provide important information to leadership about the important benefits of the Innovators, efforts are being made to document important outcomes of the Innovator program at Ohio State University. Currently, an IRB approved study is being conducted to measure the actual engagement of those enrolled in the Innovator program. The research questions include: (a) Are there demographic differences among Wellness Innovators who are engaged or disengaged in the Wellness Innovator program?; and (b) Are there perceived differences in direct manager support among Wellness Innovators that are engaged or disengaged in the Wellness Innovator program? These are important questions to ask to help practitioners lead wellness teams that effectively accomplish their roles and responsibilities. In the survey, questions such as "How engaged are you in communicating wellness information, activities, resources, and events with your department/colleagues?" "What factors influence your decision to remain engaged in the Wellness Innovator program?" "What is/was your biggest barrier to facilitating wellness in your department?"; demographic information is being collected to understand these dedicated individuals more fully. In addition, assessments are being gathered to determine the impact of the Innovators on their colleagues' healthy lifestyle beliefs and behaviors.

CRITICISM OF H&W PROGRAMS

Before you get too excited about starting your health and wellness champions network, keep in mind that employee health and wellness programs are not always perceived in a positive light. Crafting such a program means *defining* health and wellness. When companies do that, they open the door to discriminatory health judgments. These decisions can do the exact opposite of what you want your champions network to accomplish by negatively affecting employee engagement. A common criticism of such programs: a company that really cares about its employees' health would just provide better health benefits packages. Here are some other criticisms of corporate health and wellness programs, as provided by Workable:

> Before you get too excited about starting your health and wellness champions network, keep in mind that employee health and wellness programs are not always perceived in a positive light.

They use faulty metrics to measure health.

Traditional programs use metrics that are not always accurate. For example, biometric screenings are a popular feature of most wellness programs and include calculating a person's body mass index (BMI) to determine obesity, however, research suggests that BMI is an ineffective measurement of healthy weight.

They are "all stick and no carrot."

Wellness programs are often a way to shift health costs onto employees. Employers often promote these programs and their financial incentives as optional, but in some workplaces, there's a non-participation fee: higher health premiums. Penalizing employees who don't sign up for a wellness program can send the wrong message.

They compromise health privacy.

Corporate wellness programs bring health privacy concerns to the forefront. Under new U.S. Equal Employment Opportunity Commission rules, companies can require employees to share health data to obtain a financial incentive as part of a program—or pay higher premiums. This heavy-handed approach puts older workers who might have serious medical conditions in an uncomfortable position.

No one's sure they work.

Wellness program success is all over the map. Some cases show they don't reduce health costs or improve employees' health, and half of employers who offer wellness programs don't formally evaluate them. Most employers said their programs reduced health costs, absenteeism, and health-related productivity losses; however, some studies have shown that only 2 percent could provide actual savings estimates.

So, does this mean you should scrap your idea of building a best-in-class champions network to help reinforce your company's health and wellness program? Not at all. It does mean you need to do your research *prior* to setting up such a network. Have you considered some of the criticisms mentioned above while designing your network? Do you know whether the existing culture of your organization will embrace such a network, or might it be perceived negatively? Even if there are aspects of a traditional corporate wellness program that would be viewed unfavorably, what positive characteristics of such a program could be reinforced through a champions network?

For example, you may want to establish a champions network that supports a culture of wellness without forcing health requirements on employees or being overly intrusive into employees' privacy. Consider these options and consult with other internal stakeholders (for example, Human Resources) as you move forward with your plans to establish an H&W champions network in your organization.

Let's now turn to our third type of champions network—increasingly popular but controversial in some circles—Environmental and Social Responsibility.

*"You cannot escape the responsibility of tomorrow
by evading it today."*

ABRAHAM LINCOLN, U.S. PRESIDENT

11

ENVIRONMENTAL AND SOCIAL
RESPONSIBILITY

A modern trend among organizations is the implementation of and investment in programs relating to a range of environmental and social issues. Previously labeled CSR (corporate social responsibility), such initiatives now fall under the label of ESG (environment, social, and governance). Below is an excerpt of an argument in support of the ESG movement from Andrew Winston, a leading author on sustainable business strategies:

> *"Companies can't sit on the sidelines anymore because, well, there are no sidelines. In a transparent world, your silence will speak volumes.*

> *"Of course, these are choppy waters to navigate. But for your stakeholders, your consistency becomes very valuable. You can't say you stand for equity and then stay silent when the government moves to curtail the rights of many of your employees or customers. Likewise, you shouldn't have aggressive carbon-reduction goals, but then lobby against any government action to reduce emissions.*

> *"Your connection to a party and its philosophies is no longer just about tax rates or special industry incentives or laws. As the culture wars have heated up, it's been good for politicians with populist leanings to attack business—from all*

sides. So, assess what will really help your company and sector move down a more just and net positive path, to meet your big carbon-reduction goals, and to protect your vulnerable employees and customers."

The recent push for ESG programs and initiatives in the workplace has in turn been countered by an anti-ESG movement. Notable critics, including business magnate Elon Musk, have called the ESG movement *"a scam"* that has been *"weaponized by phony social justice warriors."* Other ESG opponents such as Heritage Foundation President Kevin Roberts have gone as far as labeling the movement *"a clear and present danger to the American way of life, the soul of our nation, and every sector of our economy."*

> Whatever your opinion of it, ESG seems to be here to stay.

In the end, the opinions of many ESG opponents may prove to be irrelevant, as more companies (as well as their customers and shareholders) are placing greater emphasis on ESG initiatives. As well, a younger generation of employees is weighing the strength of companies' ESG profiles in making their employment decisions.

Whatever your opinion of it, ESG seems to be here to stay. If you have the support of your leadership, numerous ESG ideas, programs, and initiatives can be spread throughout your organization using the champions network model. In this chapter we'll discuss two different categories of ESG within the context of champions-network development: environmental sustainability and diversity, equity, and inclusion (DEI).

ENVIRONMENTAL SUSTAINABILITY

Building an environmental sustainability champions network can be difficult if an organization doesn't already have a commitment to sustainability. The good news is that an increasing number of organizations have begun to prioritize sustainability as part of their ESG efforts. A champions network helps to supplement an organization's existing commitment to sustainability, or it can be the first step in demonstrating a sustainability commitment within the organization.

Environmental sustainability champions traverse regions, departments, and seniority levels to drive sustainability efforts and create greater awareness of and engagement with sustainability programs and initiatives across the organization. Sustainability champions help to make their colleagues aware of environmental issues being faced by the organization, work to develop tangible strategies to tackle such issues, and take meaningful action to cut down on their organization's carbon footprint and address climate change concerns. In other words, being a sustainability champion is about much more than reminding employees to celebrate Earth Day!

Below is a list of the benefits associated with an Environmental Sustainability champions network, followed by a list of sustainability ideas, both provided by PlanetMark:

- Achieving reductions in carbon emissions.
- Finding savings associated with energy, waste, water, and travel costs.
- Changing behaviors and attitudes toward environmental sustainability.
- Bringing people from different parts of the company together to collaborate.
- Allowing employees across the organization to learn new skills and knowledge regarding environmental sustainability in the workplace.
- Creating fully engaged and informed employees. This leads to employees who feel more valued, show increased productivity, enjoy a better work environment, and possess a greater sense of loyalty to their organization (as you probably know by now, this is the case for *any* champions network).

Sustainability Ideas for a Champions Network

✓ Encourage positive behavior changes, such as turning off lights and equipment when not in use or taking part in the company's recycling programs.

- ✓ Set up friendly competitions to encourage behavior changes that promote sustainable practices.
- ✓ Communicate sustainability messages, including new policies, initiatives, and reports that may impact the workforce and the company overall.
- ✓ Run workshops, events, training, and meetings on sustainability topics.
- ✓ Support data-gathering efforts to analyze and improve carbon footprints.
- ✓ Generate ideas for local sustainability improvements and initiatives.
- ✓ Help explain complex sustainability terms or concepts to colleagues.
- ✓ Focus on quick wins and early successes to encourage longer-term actions.
- ✓ Recognize the efforts of individual employees who take on leadership roles in sustainability initiatives.
- ✓ Ensure that the sustainability initiatives and ideas of the champions network align with the greater sustainability goals and objectives of the organization.
- ✓ Encourage employees to come up with their own creative sustainability ideas.
- ✓ Bring in outside sustainability experts to share their knowledge and stories.

Amazon Sustainability Ambassadors

Excerpt from:
"Sustainability Ambassadors"
Amazon

Sustainability Ambassadors are sustainability-minded Amazon employees who work to amplify global, company-wide efforts at the local level. Ambassadors lead projects on Amazon campuses and create virtual engagement opportunities to inspire fellow employees, both at work and at home. The program also serves as a community for sharing best practices among teams in different settings and locations.

Driving Local Impact, Globally

Since launching in 2018, the Sustainability Ambassador program has transformed into a collaborative network across 1,250 global locations.

In 2021, we launched new chapters in India, Brazil, Australia, Mexico, the United Arab Emirates, and beyond.

Ambassadors who work at physical sites, like fulfillment centers, focus on opportunities to engage fellow employees through on-site initiatives. Ambassadors in our corporate offices are focused on sustainability initiatives that can be done virtually in any setting.

Singapore

Ambassadors in Singapore led a tree-planting event to support the Singapore Botanic Gardens.

U.S.

Ambassadors at a facility in Wisconsin partnered with a local waste vendor to install recycling stations for employees to deposit used electronics.

In Tennessee, more than 35 Ambassadors hosted an event at a nearby middle school and planted 44 trees that will help sequester carbon and divert stormwater at the school campus.

Italy

In Italy, an Ambassador spearheaded an effort to include sustainability information in new hire orientation programming for thousands of new Amazon employees.

DIVERSITY, EQUITY, AND INCLUSION

Falling within the "S" of ESG, diversity, equity, and inclusion (DEI) are three closely linked values held by many modern organizations that work to be supportive of different groups of individuals, including people of different races, ethnicities, religions, abilities, genders, and sexual orientations. Over the past few years, many organizations have taken strides to build diversity, equity, and inclusion into their policies, hiring practices, and corporate initiatives—including DEI champions networks. Before looking at a real-world example, let's briefly review what DEI is and the benefits it can bring to an organization.

DEI Defined

Diversity, equity, and inclusion are often grouped together because they are interconnected, but they are also easily misunderstood. Below is a summary of the individual meanings and implications of each of these terms, as provided by McKinsey & Company:

Diversity

Diversity refers to who is represented in the workforce. Some examples of diversity in workplaces include:

- Gender diversity: What amount of men, women, and nonbinary people make up a given population?
- Age diversity: Are people in a group from mostly one generation, or is there a mix of ages?
- Ethnic diversity: Do people in a group share common national or cultural traditions, or do they represent different backgrounds?
- Physical ability and neurodiversity: Are the perspectives of people with disabilities, whether apparent or not, accounted for?

Equity

Equity refers to fair treatment for all people, so that the norms, practices, and policies in place ensure identity is not predictive of opportunities or workplace outcomes. Equity differs from equality in a subtle but important way. While equality assumes that all people should be treated the same, equity takes into consideration a person's unique circumstances, adjusting treatment accordingly so that the end result is equal.

Inclusion

Inclusion refers to how the workforce experiences the workplace. This includes the degree to which organizations embrace all employees and enable them to make meaningful contributions. Companies intent on recruiting a diverse workforce strive to develop a sufficiently inclusive culture where all employees can make their voices heard.

> Research has shown a correlation between improved business performance and diversity, with greater access to talent and increased employee engagement contributing to this performance effect.

> "You don't need to call it DEI, you can call it whatever you want—I call it good business. It means taking the people that you're selling to and making sure your workforce looks like them, and making sure you can reflect their values and being able to connect to that. That's what works for me."
>
> **Mark Cuban**, Entrepreneur and Investor

Why Is DEI Important in the Workplace?

Research has shown a correlation between improved business performance and diversity, with greater access to talent and increased employee engagement contributing to this performance effect. In addition, DEI strategies significantly affect an organization's overall performance in the following ways, as provided by McKinsey & Company:

- *Winning talent*: Organizations that monitor the demographic pro-file of their workforces are better able to retain top performers while making sure diverse talent isn't lost.
- *Improving the quality of decision making*: Diversity brings multi-ple perspectives to the table during times when enhanced problem-solving skills and vision are needed.
- *Increasing customer insight and innovation*: Diverse teams are typi-cally more innovative and better at anticipating shifts.
- *Driving employee motivation and satisfaction*: Research shows that companies that are committed to diversity are 75 percent more likely to report a pro-teamwork culture.
- *Improving a company's global image and license to operate*: Companies that maintain or increase their focus on inclusion and diver-sity during crises are poised to avoid consequences such as struggling to attract talent or losing customers and govern-ment support.

Accessibility Champions Networks

There are many types of DEI champions networks, including acces-sibility networks. Accessibility networks help spread the message and support initiatives focused on ways to meet the needs of disabled people in order to create more accessible products and services. An example of such a network operates at one of the largest technology companies in the world: Google.

Google Accessibility Champions

Excerpt from:
"Champions of Accessibility"
AbilityNet

How Google runs its champions network

Google's champions' network began as small groups of evangelists but has become a more structured network aligned to organizational goals.

Christopher Patnoe, Head of Accessibility and Disability Inclusion EMEA [at] Google, took inspiration from a colleague's jiu-jitsu experience to create ideas around a black belt in accessibility. Patnoe developed a structure based around belts and levels, and the concept of the dojo applied to roles within Google.

"We took disparate groups of designers and engineers and program managers who wanted to do the right thing, and we helped teach them how to think about it. As a result, we created this concept called 'the dojo,'" said Patnoe.

Patnoe added, "There are different dojos, [such as an] engineering dojo and a designer dojo. They need to learn different things, and we prioritize different things for each of them.

"A program manager's dojo would be different from a tech writer's dojo, but they all have the dojo as a common language."

Right now, the dojo has around 1,200 members in total, with about 350 of those rising through the ranks every year, demonstrating strong levels of engagement.

Motivating champions using the model of "the dojo"

The dojo concept encourages champions to develop their expertise over time and helps ensure that they stay within the network.

"When we started, it was hard to motivate people," said Patnoe, "because they'd do a couple of things and then they'd get busy, they'd go and do something else. So having this idea of a black belt keeps people going."

Patnoe is clear that building a champions' network has its challenges.

It takes time, it takes resources and—ideally—it takes a budget. Obstacles crop up all the time, and progress isn't always linear or direct.

"It's sometimes three steps forward, two steps back. There's always progress, but sometimes it's not as easy as you want it to be. People will leave, and you have to train new people."

However, Patnoe believes it's worth it and hopes to extend the network to cover new parts of the organization, including the sales team.

"I'd love to train 1,000 salespeople in accessibility and then have them include Google's accessibility mission and the tools that we have as part of their sales pitch. And see if we could have accessibility be a factor in increasing sales. That would be really cool."

Developing your champions network

It also helps that Google has a policy where employees can focus on a project outside their primary responsibilities for 20 percent of their time. Accessibility projects fit under this umbrella and are recognized as a citizenship goal.

"The fact that we have so many accessibility teams and such momentum inside Google on accessibility is the direct result of the passion of people in the champs' network," said Patnoe.

He said, "[They] take it seriously, seeing it as a career opportunity, an opportunity to give back to themselves or give back in honor of someone that they love. Or just because it's a really cool problem that you get to solve."

Patnoe believes that it's always possible to do accessibility better.

"You're never going to get it completely right," he said. "But where you don't have a team, the champs' network is the de facto team. These are the people who are doing everything they can to make the products accessible.

"Their job, when it goes well, is to become that accessibility team. Then they really get to have the influence because they have management support, have the headcount, and work on a full-time rather than a part-time basis. I really see this as being the earth in which you grow that team."

Many organizations today are investing in consultants and experts to advise on ESG strategies, carbon reduction initiatives, and the wide-scale implementation of programs that focus on diversity, equity, and inclusion practices. So why not also consider a more *cost-effective* approach to supporting ESG initiatives in the form of a champions network? An ESG champions network allows an organization to leverage its existing workforce, creating awareness and action around big ideas in sustainability, racial justice, community involvement, and much more.

"You need to have a collaborative hiring process."

STEVE JOBS, CEO OF APPLE

12

EMPLOYEE RECRUITMENT AND RETENTION

Studies have shown that the younger generation of job candidates are more likely to take one job over another based on personal relationships formed during the recruiting process. However, recruiters can't be expected to manage and build personal relationships with *all* prospective candidates. So how do recruiters develop these personal relationships that are sought after by Millennial and Gen Z jobseekers? You guessed it: champions networks. With virtual recruiting becoming more popular, the implementation of such networks is more relevant now than ever.

Who are these champions? Potentially, any non-recruiter within your organization can be used to engage candidates. In many cases, these can be employees in the same role or department that the candidate is interested in, although that isn't necessarily a requirement. Regardless of who they are, Recruitment and Retention (R&R) champions should be viewed as an extension of your

> The younger generation of job candidates are more likely to take one job over another based on personal relationships formed during the recruiting process.

organization's Human Resources team and supplemental to the recruiting process.

Ideally, the value of such champions goes beyond the recruitment process. Once a new employee is hired, the relationships that are built during the recruitment process often extend through employment, serving as a catalyst for career development and mentorship.

GOALS OF AN R&R NETWORK

Your R&R champions serve to support the recruitment process, becoming messengers of the organization's culture and proactively developing relationships with candidates to increase the chances of great candidates accepting job offers. Like all other champions networks discussed so far, R&R champions don't replace the experts (the recruiters and HR professionals); they provide support and, in some cases, ease the burden on overwhelmed recruiting teams. R&R champions may be tasked with answering candidate questions, discussing company culture, or providing specific information to candidates regarding work-life balance, advancement opportunities, or workplace inclusivity—the role of an R&R champion can be as narrow or broad as their training dictates.

FINDING THE RIGHT R&R CHAMPIONS

Your R&R champions should love where they work. They should be excited to talk to job candidates and motivated to bring talented individuals into the organization. More than any other type of champion discussed in this book, R&R champions need to be willing to participate in events and activities outside of normal working hours. This could include job fairs, recruiting sessions, or a weekend phone call with a job candidate. Of course, you are looking for champions with diverse backgrounds and experiences that are reflective of your candidate pool—professional expertise, educational background, regional differences, age, gender, orientation, race, etc. In recruiting your R&R

champions, make clear to them the value they are providing in helping to bring in talent and shape the organization for years to come.

STUDENT R&R AMBASSADORS

While R&R networks are frequently utilized in the corporate world, they have also become ubiquitous at many colleges and universities that are looking to attract new students. The following is one example of a student ambassador program that is reflective of many networks of its kind at institutions of higher education. Whether it's in a corporate or educational context, the goal of such networks is generally the same: attract new talent by leveraging your current employee/student base to help *champion* your organization.

Bruin Ambassadors

Excerpt from:
"Bruin Ambassadors"
UCLA Undergraduate Admission

Would you like to share the Bruin spirit with younger students in and around Los Angeles? If so, you might be a perfect match for the Bruin Ambassador program.

About the Program

The Bruin Ambassador Program is a team of current UCLA students employed by the office of Undergraduate Admission. Ambassadors play a key role in the recruitment of future Bruins from high schools across Southern California. This is an exciting paid position with opportunities to build your resume, work with prospective students, and gain professional experience for your career.

Responsibilities

Ambassador duties include participation in the following types of events:

- Ambassadors conduct admission presentations and application workshops at high schools across LA County. Ambassadors will share their UCLA experiences and be trained on the UCLA freshman admission process
- College fairs
- On-campus admission presentations
- On-campus student panels
- Special social media projects
- Admission events including UC Counselor Conferences, UCLA Open House, UCLA Bruin Day (Freshman and Transfer), STOMP Conference, UCLA Experience and more
- Committees
- Weekly office hours
- Weekly meetings on Tuesdays from 6 p.m. - 7 p.m. during the school year (fall, winter, and spring quarters)

Requirements

- Must be responsible, articulate, flexible, and committed
- Must be detail-oriented and work well independently
- Must be comfortable speaking in front of large groups
- Familiarity with the UCLA campus, knowledge of admission procedures, and general knowledge of academic requirements and helpful resources
- Experience practicing the above qualifications is preferred
- Must be comfortable driving in Los Angeles (may travel to Ventura, San Bernardino, Riverside and/or Orange Counties)
- Desire to join a diverse team of leaders across campus
- Desire to work with prospective students from first-generation, low-income, and disadvantaged neighborhoods

As with any other type of champions network, the R&R network can backfire if champions are not properly trained and if the network is not well executed. Unfortunately, I encountered this firsthand at a large and well-known technology company where I interviewed. The company proudly advertised an Employee Ambassadors Program to its job candidates, offering hundreds of ambassadors willing to talk to candidates about their experience working at the company.

The first ambassador I reached out to never responded. The second ambassador responded, but only to apologize and tell me that his schedule would not allow him to speak with me. The third (and final) ambassador I reached out to seemed less than thrilled with his current job situation and the overall company culture. In the end, my decision not to pursue the opportunity was an easy one to make. If I couldn't find three people willing to recommend the employer, how could I be confident that choosing it as my new "home" for the next decade would be a good decision?

"It always seems impossible until it's done."

NELSON MANDELA, PRESIDENT OF SOUTH AFRICA

CONCLUSION

As I finished the manuscript for this book, I began to look into marketing strategies for authors. I came across a virtual webinar advertised as the definitive guide to *"increase book sales and grow your author brand!"*

The webinar began with some lessons learned by the speaker:

"I did things the wrong way at first, so don't make the same mistakes I made . . ."

It ended as most free webinars do, with a hard sell:

"If you like what you learned today and want to take it to the next level, give us your credit card number and register for our VIP course, for the low price of only . . ."

While the end of the webinar turned into a high-pressure sales pitch that would make a used car salesman blush, somewhere in the middle of the webinar the speaker caught my attention. Specifically, his advice on how to *influence* others to read your book:

"Traditional advertising is no longer the way to get your book in the hands of the most people. If you want to get your book out there . . . build a network of little Oprahs."

You're probably familiar with Oprah's Book Club and the impact that an endorsement can have on book sales. Just receiving Oprah Winfrey's stamp of approval is enough to catapult the average book into best-selling status—a phenomenon that has come to be known as "The Oprah Effect."

The speaker's advice (assuming you don't have a direct connection to Oprah) was to develop *"a network of little Oprahs."* Meaning, find people who you know are trusted and influential, then ask them to read your book and recommend it. In other words: build a champions network.

The words of Greg Satell—renowned author and advisor on creating organizational change—may best summarize the advice and concepts discussed in this book:

> *"People tend to notice transformation once it's already happened, and often get the impression that because it became big that it started that way. That's almost never true. Initiatives become transformative through building success upon success. You don't need to convince everybody all at once. You need to start with a small group that's enthusiastic about change. That one small principle can make a big difference."*

While we often seek organizational change through leadership directives, the implementation of new policies, or the advice of outside "experts," common sense and experience (along with over 100 years of sociological research) tell us that significant and sustainable change does not come from the top down, nor from the outside. The most effective way to expand your influence is to leverage your existing networks and find those who will champion your ideas at the local level—in time, spreading them throughout your organization. After all, a change in culture isn't achieved by a mandate, but through a movement.

Activate your network of champions.

RESOURCES

Introduction

- Gallo, Carmine. "The Art of Persuasion Hasn't Changed in 2,000 Years." *Harvard Business Review*, August 6, 2019. https://hbr.org/2019/07/the-art-of-persuasion-hasnt-changed-in-2000-years.

Chapter 1 – The Psychology of a Champions Network

- Cullen, Kristin L., Charles J. Palus, and Craig Appaneal. Developing Network Perspective: Understanding the Basics of Social Networks and Their Role in Leadership. White paper. Center for Creative Leadership. https://doi.org/10.35613/ccl.2014.1019.
- Rogers, Everett M., Arvind Singhal, and Margaret M. Quinlan. Diffusion of Innovations, 5th ed. Free Press, 2003.
- Berger, Jonah. *How Ideas Spread: Course Guidebook*. The Great Courses, 2014.
- Baer, Markus. "Putting Creativity to Work: The Implementation of Creative Ideas in Organizations." *The Academy of Management Journal* 55, no. 5 (2012): 1102-19. http://www.jstor.org/stable/23412455.

Chapter 2 – What Is a Champions Network?

- "A Guide to Building your Program Champion Network." Aduro. https://adurolife.com/blog/employee-well-being/build-champion-network-program-to-boos t-wellbeing-program-engagement/.
- Warrick, D.D. "Developing Organization Change Champions." *OD Practitioner* 41, no. 1 (2009): 14-19.
- Howell, Jane M., and Christine M. Shea. "Effects of Champion Behavior, Team Potency, and External Communication Activities on Predicting Team Performance." *Group & Organization Management* 31, no. 2 (2006): 180-211. https://doi.org/10.1177/1059601104273067.

Chapter 3 – Gaining Leadership Commitment

- Silverman, Matthew. "Developing a Trade Compliance Champions Network." Presentation at 2022 ICPA Summer Conference, Paradise Island, Bahamas, June 7, 2022.

Chapter 4 – Creating the Network Structure

- Bailey, Julia, and Matt Silverman. "Optimizing the Structure of Your Ambassadors Program to Maximize Effectiveness." Presentation at SCCE Leading an Effective Ethics and Compliance Ambassadors Program, Virtual, December 8, 2022.

Chapter 5 – Recruiting the Champions

- "Recruit Champions to Support Your Big Change." Davis & Company, https://www.davisandco.com/guide/recruit-champions-support-your-big-change.
- "Build an Ambassador Network: Unify Your People Worldwide by Recruiting Local Ambassadors." Benevity. https://benevity.com/hubfs/B-Hive%20assets/Benevity_Ambassador_Guide_.pdf.

- Steinholtz, Ruth, and Jennifer Selliers. "Recruiting and Training Your Ambassadors: It's All About the People." Presentation at SCCE Leading an Effective Ethics and Compliance Ambassadors Program, Virtual, August 18, 2022.

Chapter 6 – Training the Champions

- Feser, Claudio. *When Execution Isn't Enough: Decoding Inspirational Leadership,* 1st ed. Wiley, 2016.
- Grant, Adam (@AdamMGrant). "The irony of 'soft skills' is that they're often the hardest to master." Twitter, August 12, 2021. https://twitter.com/AdamMGrant/status/1425946948322742274.

Chapter 7 – Implementing the Network

- Bliss, Roz, and Kay Chapman. "Inspiring, Sustaining and Expanding the Network in the Medium and Long Term: Building in Continuous Improvement." Presentation at SCCE Leading an Effective Ethics and Compliance Ambassadors Program, Virtual, August 18, 2022.
- "Digital Champions Network." Our Projects and Schemes, Digital Kent. https://www.digitalkent.uk/information/projects/dcn.

Chapter 8 – Measuring Network Success

- Jha, Renu, and Duncan Milne. "Metrics and Assessing Program's Effectiveness." Presentation at SCCE Leading an Effective Ethics and Compliance Ambassadors Program, Virtual, August 18, 2022.

Chapter 9 – Compliance and Ethics

- Silverman, Matt. "'Championing' Your Compliance Program." Compliance Cosmos, November 2020. https://compliancecosmos.org/championing-your-compliance-program.
- Fine, Lisa, and Duncan Milne. "Communicating with the Wider Workforce." Presentation at SCCE Leading an Effective Ethics and Compliance Ambassadors Program, Virtual, August 18, 2022.
- "Compliance Champions." 3BL Media. https://www.3blmedia.com/news/compliance-champions.
- Milne, Duncan. "Compliance Champions Can Help You Drive a Stronger Compliance Culture." Compliance Cosmos, May 2020. https://compliancecosmos.org/compliance-champions-can-help-you-drive-stronger-compliance-culture.
- "Compliance Champions Considerations Checklist." Spark Compliance Consulting. Handout. "Wildly Successful International Compliance Champion Programs: Making Them Great." SCCE 21st Annual Compliance & Ethics Institute, Phoenix, Arizona, October 18, 2022.
- "Developing Freedom to Speak Up Champion and Ambassador Networks: Guidance for Freedom to Speak Up Guardians." National Guardian's Office, April 2021. https://nationalguardian.org.uk/wp-content/uploads/2021/04/Guidance-on-Champions-and-Ambassador-Networks-2021.pdf.
- "Engaging Ethical Ambassadors on the Front Lines." Notre Dame Deloitte Center for Ethical Leadership. https://ethicalleadership.nd.edu/news/on-the-front-lines/.
- "Evaluation of Corporate Compliance Programs." U.S. Department of Justice. https://www.justice.gov/criminal-fraud/page/file/937501/download.
- "Federal Sentencing Guidelines Manual." United States Sentencing Commission. https://www.ussc.gov/guidelines/archive/2004-federal-sentencing-guidelines-manual.

- "Guide for Building and Sustaining an Effective Champion Program." Business Ethics Leadership Alliance. https://ethisphere.com/resources/champion-guide/.
- "Compliance." Cambridge Dictionary. https://dictionary.cambridge.org/us/dictionary/english/compliance.
- "Ethics." Merriam-Webster Dictionary. https://www.merriam-webster.com/dictionary/ethic.
- "People Power Extending the Reach of Corporate Compliance & Ethics." MHP. https://mhp.com.ua/en/corporate-ethics-and-compliance/mhp-compliance-ambassadors-program.
- Colling, Beth, and Toni-Lynne Langeveld. "Successfully Navigating the Changing Landscape for Ambassador Programs." Compliance Cosmos, December 2022. https://compliancecosmos.org/successfully-navigating-changinglandscape-ambassadorprograms-12082022-0.
- Fox, Thomas R. "The Compliance Champion: Getting People to Solve Problems Without You." JDSUPRA, September 13, 2011. https://www.jdsupra.com/legalnews/the-compliance-champion-getting-people-90581/.
- Murphy, Joseph E. "Using Incentives in Your Compliance and Ethics Program." Compliance Cosmos, June 2023. https://compliancecosmos.org/using-incentives-your-compliance-and-ethics-program.

Chapter 10 – Health and Wellness

- "10 Tips for Success with Wellness Champion Networks." StayWell. https://www.shrm.org/ResourcesAndTools/hr-topics/benefits/Documents/StayWell_Tip-Sheet_FINAL.pdf.
- "Build Your Well-Being Champion Network." WebMD Health Services. https://info.webmdhealthservices.com/rs/503-BMI-508/images/WebMD%20Wellness%20Champions%20Tookit_2016.pdf.

- "Building a Wellness Champion Network." ShapeUp. https://cdn2.hubspot.net/hub/45508/file-704822506-pdf/downloads/BuildingAWellnessChampion_27Mar14.pdf.
- "Engaging Innovative Advocates as Public Health Champions." FHI 360. https://www.fhi360.org/resource/engaging-innovative-advocates-public-health-champions.
- "Starting a Wellness Program at Your Worksite." Mississippi State Department of Health. https://msdh.ms.gov/page/43,0,277,734.html.
- "The Problem with Employee Wellness Programs." Workable. https://resources.workable.com/stories-and-insights/employee-wellness-programs.
- Burger, David. "Wellness Ambassadors to Support Peer Dentists Who May Be Struggling." ADA News, November 4, 2022. https://adanews.ada.org/ada-news/2022/november/wellness-ambassadors-to-support-peer-dentists-who-maybe-struggling.
- Amaya, Megan, et. al. "Workplace Wellness Champions: Lessons Learned and Implications for Future Programming." *Building Healthy Academic Communities Journal* 1, no. 1 (2017): 59-67. https://library.osu.edu/ojs/index.php/BHAC/article/view/5744.

Chapter 11 – Environmental and Social Responsibility

- Brubaker, Richard, Mike Hager, and Charlie Matthews. *Building a Sustainability Ambassador Network*. Collective Responsibility. https://www.coresponsibility.com/wp-content/uploads/2016/05/Building-A-Sustainability-Ambassador-Network-Final-1.pdf.
- Barry, Eloise. "Why Tesla CEO Elon Musk Is Calling ESG a 'Scam.'" *Time,* May 25, 2022. https://time.com/6180638/tesla-esg-index-musk/.
- "Conservative Movement Is Winning on ESG." The Heritage Foundation, February 1, 2023. https://www.heritage.org/press/conservative-movement-winning-esg.

- Schuster, Simon. "'Call Me Woke,' Mark Cuban Says on Mackinac Island." MLive, May 31, 2023. https://www.mlive. com/politics/2023/05/call-me-woke-mark-cuban-says-on-mackinac-island.html.
- "Champions of Accessibility." AbilityNet. https://abilitynet.org.uk/accessibility-services/ building-accessibility-champions-network.
- "Corporate Responsibility Champions Network: A 'How to' Guide." Doughty Centre. https://dspace.lib.cranfield.ac.uk/ handle/1826/3796.
- "Sustainability Ambassadors." Amazon. https:// sustainability.aboutamazon.com/society/employees/ sustainability-ambassadors.
- "Sustainability Champion Role Description." University of Kent. https://www.kent.ac.uk/sustainability/futureproof/ sustainability-champions.
- "Sustainability Champions Guide." PlanetMark, 2021. https://www.planetmark.com/wp-content/uploads/2022/01/ Guide-Setting-Up-A-Sustainability-Champions-Programme.pdf.
- "What Is Diversity, Equity, and Inclusion?" McKinsey & Company, August 17, 2022. https://www.mckinsey. com/featured-insights/mckinsey-explainers/ what-is-diversity-equity-and-inclusion.
- Winston, Andrew. "Why Business Leaders Must Reject the Anti-ESG Movement." *Harvard Business Review,* April 5, 2023. https://hbr.org/2023/04/ why-business-leaders-must-resist-the-anti-esg-movement.

Chapter 12 – Employee Recruitment and Retention

- "Ambassador Program Playbook." Handshake. https:// joinhandshake.com/wp-content/uploads/2022/04/ HS_AmbassadorProgramPlaybook-compressed.pdf.
- "Bruin Ambassadors." UCLA Undergraduate Admission. https://admission.ucla.edu/contact/bruin-ambassadors.

Conclusion

- "How Oprah's Book Club Came to Be." Oprah. com. https://www.oprah.com/oprahsbookclub/ how-oprahs-book-club-came-to-be.
- Satell, Greg. "To Implement Change, You Don't Need to Convince Everyone at Once." *Harvard Business Review*, May 11, 2023. https://hbr.org/2023/05/ to-implement-change-you-dont-need-to-convince-everyone-at-once.

ABOUT THE AUTHOR

 Matt Silverman is a speaker, attorney, and the founder and CEO of The Blueprint Organization, a consulting firm dedicated to building champions networks.

As an international trade lawyer, Matt has worked in the U.S. Senate, global law firms, and Fortune 500 companies in the technology, telecommunications, aerospace, defense, and energy industries.

Matt is a sought-after speaker on topics ranging from international law and compliance to influence and champions-network development. He is a frequent contributor to industry publications, podcasts, and conferences. His bimonthly column, "Keeping Perspective," is published in *Compliance and Ethics Professional (CEP) Magazine*.

Originally from Evanston, Illinois, Matt now lives with his family in Arizona.

Matt can be reached by email at matt@blueprintorg.com.

LOOKING TO BUILD A CHAMPIONS NETWORK?

The Blueprint Organization is dedicated to building and improving champions networks by utilizing advisors with subject-matter expertise in areas such as corporate compliance, antitrust, fraud prevention, DEI, health and wellness, ethics, customer experience, alcohol regulation, hospitality, global trade, and more. Founded by Matt Silverman, The Blueprint Organization provides customized program materials, resources, and training that fit the individual goals of its clients. If you're looking to build a new champions network or improve an existing network, contact Matt at matt@blueprintorg.com or visit https://blueprintorg.com.

BOOK MATT SILVERMAN TO SPEAK

Matt accepts a limited number of annual speaking engagements. To book Matt to speak, email him at matt@blueprintorg.com or visit https://mattsblueprint.com.

HOW YOU CAN CHAMPION THIS BOOK

Dear Reader,

I hope that you enjoyed this book and found it valuable. If so, here's how you can help me spread the word:

If you know of others who might benefit from this book, consider buying them a copy as a gift.

If you'd like to purchase copies of this book for your team or organization, bulk discounts are available by contacting me directly at matt@blueprintorg.com.

Finally, please consider leaving an online review anywhere that this book is available for purchase.

Thank you!

MATT SILVERMAN

Printed in the USA
CPSIA information can be obtained
at www.ICGtesting.com
LVHW092349130924
790714LV00001B/2

9 781956 531107